The MBLEx (Massage & Bodywork Licensing Examination) is governed by the Federation of State Massage Therapy Boards (FSMTB). It is designed to provide a standard examination for students of Massage for entry-level professional scope of practice in gaining licensure. The FSMTB was established in 2005 with the intent to build a support system for the Member Boards. Their goals from the beginning were to work towards cooperation in implementing regulations and procedures for the requirements to establish safe and effective Massage Therapy and Bodywork practices.

The MBLEx is not set up to trick or deceive the test taker. There is only one real answer to a test question. You will have 2.5 hours to answer 125 multiple-choice questions. If you take breaks your time doesn't stop. The examination is scored on a scale starting at 300 and ending at 900. A passing score of 630 implies a minimum standard for competent practice as a Massage Therapist. The diagnostic information for each category and your numbered score will be given to you at the testing center when your exam is completed.

The exam has eight concentrated areas of content: Client assessment and treatment plans, Benefits and Affects of Techniques, Pathology with Contraindications and Cautions, Massage History, Ethics- Boundaries--Laws & Regulations, Guidelines for Professional Practice, Kinesiology, Anatomy & Physiology. The Content Outline for the MBLEx breaks down further the categories used for establishing the questions in the MBLEx.

The breakdown of the massage questions on the MBLEx is as follows:

20-22 questions on Client Assessment and Treatment Plans--17% (Assessment)
20-22 questions on Benefits and Affects of Techniques--17% (Application)
15-17 questions on Pathology with Contraindications and Cautions--13% (Pathology)
5-7 questions on Massage History--5% (CAM)
15-18 questions on Ethics, Boundaries, Laws & Regulation--13% (Professional)
11-13 questions on Guidelines for Professional Practice--10% (Professional)
12-15 questions on Kinesiology 11%--(A&P)
16-18 questions on Anatomy & Physiology--14% (A&P/Body Systems)
for a total of 125 questions on each exam.

D1306699

MBLEx Fees: $195.00.
If you fail the exam you will have to apply and pay the fees if you want to take the test again.

The MBLEx has the following approximate weight for each category:
Assessment: 17% or 21 questions
Applications: 17% or 21 questions
Pathology: 13% or 16 questions
History (CAM): 5% or 6 questions
Professional: 23% or 28 questions
A&P/Kinesio/Body: 25% or 28 questions

This breakdown allows you to see where the MBLEx focuses their content, creating a focus for your studies. The highest concentration is in the A&P/Kinesio/Body and Professional sections, followed closely by the Assessment and Application (as it should be). The Pathology and history questions are helpful to know, giving you the knowledge of your client's conditions so that you are able to make connections on how the massage history affects the professional community as a whole today. When you are studying with us, it is important to note the content weight in order to better prepare yourself for the exam.

To use our site effectively it is best to review the content of your graded exams. When you have finished your practice test and have received your score, don't stop there. Check each incorrectly answered question and find out why you missed it. Was it because you didn't read the question correctly or missed one qualifying word? If you answered the question correctly, it is important to read the rationale, there may be further insights that can help you in the long run with a deeper understanding about the subject, or an easier way to remember the content.

When reviewing your tests, make sure you are breaking down the questions effectively. This is the time to practice reading each word slowly. It also helps, while reading the question, to insert one of the answers into the question to see if it fits or to see if it registers with anything in your knowledge base. If you take your time on each word, focusing on the overall relevancy, you will train your brain to pick out the best possible answer. Visualize the muscle in relation to the body, see the direction of the fibers, recall the origin and the insertion (more moveable attachment) and run through the available actions of that muscle.

Practice using scrap paper to write things down. Sometimes writing them down will trigger the information you are looking for. When you take the exam at Pearson VUE they will give you paper and pencil to use while you take the exam and then they will ask for it back when the exam is complete.

It is also best in your preparations to study at least an hour each day. When you answer a question incorrectly, use that information to find a subject matter you need to learn more about. Read all about it in your books, and look it up online. Try to make deeper connections in regards to the body relationship as a whole. As you continue to do so you will find that you can recall information faster and with more accuracy.

To be qualified to take the MBLEx you must first find out if your state accepts this exam as part of your licensing requirements. If yes, then you may apply directly with the FSMTB or through your state licensing board or agency. The fee required to take the exam is $195 due with the submittal of your MBLEx application. If you apply through your state licensing board or agency you do not need to fill out and send the application to FSMTB, the board or agency will complete that process for you.

Filling out and sending in the application does not guarantee that you are accepted to take the MBLEx. You must wait for an NTS (Notice to Schedule) that will be sent directly from the FSMTB to your email. If your state board or agency has sent in your eligibility information you will get a payment voucher that you must return in order to receive the NTS. Once you have completed this process you can then set up an appointment to take the exam with Pearson VUE. You must take the exam within 90 days of receiving the NTS, or you will be required to go through the application process again, including fees. MBLEx Survey Results

The Massage-Exam.com website is a resource for basic Massage information about our online practice exams and other links to major Massage organizations. We are not affiliated with NCBTMB, FSMTB, AMTA, ABMP, IMA or AMC. Information gathered from the websites of these organizations is to help educate and inform our fellow Massage Therapists.

Tips on taking and passing the MBLEx:

These tips have been gathered from dozens of resources. They can be applied to the MBLEx as well as any test structured in the same format.

Taking the MBLEx can be a painless experience if you are prepared with the knowledge of the course material AND an understanding of what to expect of the MBLEx test itself. We have created this page to aid in answering some of the more common questions associated with taking the MBLEx. This includes facts and advice related to taking and passing the exams. It is intended to aid the MT candidate in his or her pursuit of license and registration as a Massage Therapist.

MBLEx is a Static (Summative) Test. It measures what you have learned and is a set of standardized tests with a set amount of time and a set amount of questions.

Facts you need to know about the MBLEx:

• MBLEx test questions are multiple choice with 4 potential answers. All questions are created by a team of 15 psychometricians and testing experts along with a core group of 60 subject matter experts. They created a list of all the tasks that a massage or bodywork therapist needs to be able to perform on the job. This list of tasks was then validated by several thousand practitioners (7,646). These testing experts made sure that there is only one "best" or "correct" answer and that "each incorrect answer has some level of plausibility." Additionally, each question and answer must be easily found in the MBLEx bibliography of books used in teaching Massage Therapy curriculum.

• The MBLEx is a standard CBT (Computer Based Testing) format. All testing will be performed at a computer workstation at PearsonVue testing centers all over the United States.

• The CBT (Computer Based Testing) that the MBLEx utilizes is called Static (Summative) Tests and each exam is a standardized exam. You will have 2.5 hours and 125 questions to answer in order to complete the exam and receive your results.

• The MBLEx is administered at the Pearson VUE testing center. This CBT or Computer Based Test, will deliver questions one at a time to the candidate. Your name will be displayed at the top of the screen and on the top right side will be displayed your time remaining (you also have the option of clicking on the clock icon to get rid of the time count). The progress indicator under the time will show you first the question number you are on and then the total number of questions. The bottom left of the screen shows the navigation buttons. You can choose the Previous screen, the Navigator settings, or Next screen. The Navigator button in the lower right corner opens a window that allows you to move freely around the exam questions. The Navigator window also allows you to view the question status (complete, incomplete, or unseen), and items that are marked or flagged for review.

• Items displayed in the Navigator window are sorted by question number. You can sort the questions by Question #, Status, or Flagged for Review by clicking the column heading. Click the heading once to change the current sort order from ascending to descending order; click it again to change from descending to ascending order. An arrow pointing up indicates that the column is sorted in ascending order; an arrow pointing down indicates that it is in descending order.

• When answering a question you may click on the bubble to the left of the correct answer or on the answer itself. If you click again, this will remove the selected answer.

• To flag a question for review, click the button in the upper right corner labeled Flag for Review. If you flag an item for review, a flag appears next to that item on the review screen. Review of items must be done during the testing time. You can select items for review whether you have answered them or not. To flag an item for review, use the mouse to click the Flag for Review button. A flag image appears within the flag outline when the item has been flagged for review. To un-flag the item, click the Flag for Review button again and the flag image disappears. When you reach the last item in a section, press the Next button to move to the Review Screen.

• You can move to each question within the review screen by clicking on it or selecting Review All. **Do not click on the End Review button until you are satisfied with ALL your answers. The End Review ends your exam, it is located in the lower left side of the screen.**

• There may be some questions that have a graphic displayed in order to fully answer the question correctly.

• Exam fees ($195) can be paid online at the MBLEx website, or you can print off an application and send in the fee.

• If you do not pass the exam you may fill out the MBLEx Retake Application form and send in the ($195) fee again.

• You will receive the official exam score at the Pearson VUE testing center immediately after your examination. No other report will be sent to you in the mail or email.

• The score will automatically be reported electronically to the state board that you wrote on the application, providing it is a state that accepts MBLEx scores. The score will be reported to this first state at no cost.

• If you need to have your score sent to another state board, or need another hard copy to be sent to either you or another business, you must fill out the MBLEx Mobility Form and pay $20.00 per report.

• You can find an MBLEx testing location on this page of www.personvue.com

Advice on how to take and pass the MBLEx:

The following advice has been gleaned from dozens of sources. Information contained within has been compiled from interviews with Massage Therapists who have taken and passed the exam, related Massage discussion forums, and nationally recognized test-taking authorities.

To use our site effectively it is best to review the content of your graded exams. When you have finished your practice test and have received your score, don't stop there. Check each incorrectly answered question and find out why you missed it. Was it because you didn't read the question correctly or missed one qualifying word? If you answered the question correctly or incorrectly, it is important to read the rationale, there may be further insights that can help you in the long run with a deeper understanding about the subject, or an easier way to remember the content.

When reviewing your tests, make sure you are breaking down the questions effectively. This is the time to practice reading each word slowly. It also helps, while reading the question, to insert one of the answers into the question to see if it fits or to see if it registers with anything in your knowledge base. If you take time on each word, focusing on the overall relevancy, you will train your brain to pick out the best possible answer. Visualize the muscle in relation to the body, see the direction of the fibers, recall the origin and the insertion (more moveable attachment), and run through the available actions of that muscle.

Practice using scrap paper to write things down. Sometimes writing content down will trigger the information you are looking for. When you take the exam at Pearson VUE they will give you paper and pencil or board and marker to use while the exam is taken and then ask for it back when the exam is completed.

It is also best in your preparations to study at least an hour each day. When you answer a question incorrectly, use that information to find a subject matter you need to learn more about. Read all about it in your books, and look it up online. Try to make deeper connections in regards to the body relationship as a whole. As you continue to do so you will find that you can recall information faster and with more accuracy.

Taking the MBLEx can be a painless experience if you are prepared with the knowledge of the course material AND an understanding of what to expect of the MBLEx test itself. We have created this page to aid in answering some of the more common questions associated with taking the MBLEx. This includes facts and advice related to taking and passing the exams. It is intended to aid the MT candidate in his or her pursuit of license and certification as a Massage Therapist.

MBLEx is a Static (Summative) Test. It measures what you have learned and is a set of standardized tests with a set amount of time and a set amount of questions.

Material to study for the MBLEx:

* Realistically you should have a working knowledge of all materials covered in your massage curriculum. There is no secret method to passing the Exam. The Massage-Exam Practice Testing Application will help you become familiar with the format and content of the multiple choice questions. You can solidify the concepts of massage assessment and application by studying the massage answer rationales that accompany every question.

* Even though the MBLEx has a minimum passing threshold, you should strive to learn more than just what is necessary to pass the exam. Reading the rationales that accompany every question on Massage-Exam, will help further your knowledge, open your understanding to the concepts taught from your text, build confidence in your personal abilities as a Massage Therapist, and add a strong foundation to your new career.

The days before the MBLEx:

* Be sure to eat a balanced diet and drink lots of water on the days before the massage exam. Try to include B vitamin foods in your meals like oatmeal, bananas, and raisins, and get plenty of rest.

* Do not try to cram for the massage exam. This is not an effective way of preparing for any exam. If you don't know the information you need the night before the exam, you are not going to know it after a day or night of cramming. Get some sleep or just relax the day or night before the exam instead of cramming. The rest will do more for you than frantically pouring over your textbooks and practice massage exam questions.

* Do not eat a sugar-loaded meal or drink a lot of coffee before your exam. This will only add to existing test anxiety.

* Study for your massage exam regularly over several weeks to get the best results from your test preparation.

* Download a map of the testing center location and make sure you know exactly where the test center is, and arrive early to eliminate the stress of being late. Being late for the MBLEx is not tolerated and you will have to reschedule. You must be approved and signed up for the MBLEx, you can't just walk in to the testing center and request to take the exam. You can only bring your photo ID and a couple of pencils. Scrap paper will be provided for you in the testing area along with pencils if you are in need. These items must be returned at the end of the exam. Some testing facilities may even have a locker issued to you for your personal belongings to be stored during the exam.

* Dress in multiple layers when you go to take your exam so that you can take off what is not necessary if you are too warm. The temperature of the testing center can change during the day especially if the exam is held in a seldom used room or building.

*Use the restroom before you start the exam. You are allowed to go during the exam, but take care of it sooner rather than later. You will be required to take one form of ID with you while the other stays within the testing center. It will be verified each time you leave and enter.

*You must bring two forms of ID to the exam site. One of the IDs needs to have a photo.

While taking the MBLEx:

* Use caution with questions that contain words like always, except, never, most appropriate, and other words that qualify a question. Watch out for words that put limitations on a potential answer.

* Be sure to read the entire massage question completely at least two times and then formulate the correct answer in your head before you take a look at the multiple choice answers. If you look at the choices of answers before you understand the question entirely, you may be led into choosing an incorrect answer.

* There are four possible answers to each massage question. Two of the answers can often be eliminated right away after reading the question through twice. Once these two answers are eliminated, you only need to decide which answer is the "best possible answer" between the two remaining choices.

* Don't over-think or complicate the question. Do not add elements into questions that are not already written into it. These things can cause you to overlook the basics of the question, which is usually what you are being tested on.

* When you have completed the massage exam, review and check your answers if you have time. You are given two hours and forty minutes to complete the exam, so you should have a while to review after you have completed it. There will most certainly be at least one question that you have read incorrectly. Do not spend your review time waiting out in the car for your friend to get done.

Look at the breakdown of questions. A large portion of the exam is related to Professional Ethics /Standards (23% or approximately 28 questions), and A&P/Kinesio/Body (25% or 28 questions). The assessment and application sections are close behind with 17% or approximately 21 questions each. Many students overlook this.

The MBLEx may NOT be based upon the textbook you used in your class. The exam is based upon the MBLEx Bibliography referenced materials.

• Remember, although the MBLEx exam looks at a minimum requirement to pass, nobody wants a "just made it by the skin of the teeth" therapist. Know your stuff.

• Obviously take advantage of the Massage Practice Tests here on our site. There is detailed score tracking and exam review features that let you see your strong and weak areas while you continue to take exams and improve.

Use this information when studying and preparing for your final exam. Breakdown the subject matter to understand it better:

1. Knowledge: arrange, define, duplicate, label, list, memorize, name, order, recognize, relate, recall, repeat, reproduce, state.

2. Comprehension: classify, describe, discuss, explain, express, identify, indicate, locate, recognize, report, restate, review, select, translate.

3. Application: apply, choose, demonstrate, dramatize, employ, illustrate, interpret, operate, practice, schedule, sketch, solve, use, write.

4. Analysis: analyze, appraise, calculate, categorize, compare, contrast, criticize, differentiate, discriminate, distinguish, examine, experiment, question, test.

5. Synthesis: arrange, assemble, collect, compose, construct, create, design, develop, formulate, manage, organize, plan, prepare, propose, set up, write.

6. Evaluation: appraise, argue, assess, attach, choose, compare, defend, estimate, judge, predict, rate, core, select, support, value, evaluate.

The chart below shows the increasing level of complexity of question construction.

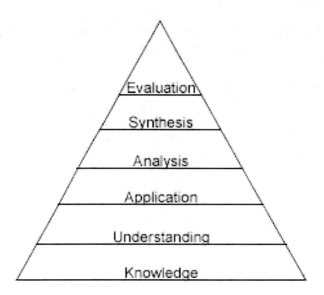

KNOWLEDGE
- Remembering;
- Memorizing;
- Recognizing;
- Recalling identification
- Recall of information
    ° Who, what, when, where, how ...?
    ° Describe

COMPREHENSION
- Interpreting;
- Translating from one medium to another;
- Describing in one's own words;
- Organization and selection of facts and ideas
    ° Retell...

APPLICATION
- Problem solving;
- Applying information to produce some result;
- Use of facts, rules, and principles;
    ° How is...an example of ...?
    ° How is...related to ...?
    ° Why is...significant?

ANALYSIS
- Subdividing something to show how it is put together;
- Finding the underlying structure of a communication;
- Identifying motives;
- Separation of a whole into component parts;
    ° What are the parts or features of ...?
    ° Classify...according to...
    ° Outline/Diagram...
    ° How does...compare/contrast with...?
    ° What evidence can you list ...?

SYNTHESIS
- Creating a unique, original product that may be in verbal form or may be a physical object;

- Combination of ideas to form a new whole;
  - ° What would you predict/infer from...?
  - ° What ideas can you add to...?
  - ° How would you create/design a new...?
  - ° What might happen if you combined...?
  - ° What solutions would you suggest for...?

EVALUATION
- Making value decisions about issues;
- Resolving controversies or differences of opinion;
- Development of opinions, judgments, or decisions
  - ° Do you agree...?
  - ° What do you think about...?
  - ° What is the most important...?
  - ° Place the following in order of priority...
  - ° How would you decide about...?
  - ° What criteria would you use to assess...?

This is the nuts and bolts of how an MBLEx exam is built. Below is an example of how an MBLEx question is constructed. This will give you some insight into the thinking behind each question.

Steps to Question Writing

A well-designed multiple-choice item consists of three main components: a stem (asks a question or poses a statement which requires completion), key (the correct answer/s), and distracter(s) (incorrect option/s). The following section is designed to enhance the candidate's understanding of the MBLEx question writing process.

Step 1. Select an area of the test plan for the focus of the item.
* Client Assessment

Step 2. Select a subcategory from the chosen area of the test plan.
* Acute injury

Step 3. Select an important concept within that subcategory.
* Assess and prioritize the injury, care, and techniques

Step 4. Use the concept selected and write the stem.
* Client worked in yard yesterday and their right lower back is in spasms
What are the first questions that need to be answered?

Step 5. Write a key to represent important information the entry-level EMT should know.
* Pain scale, use of hydrotherapy, pain medications, and restricted movements
~ ROM is stopped at the pain, don't let client push through the acute injury pain

Step 6. Identify common errors, misconceptions, or irrelevant information.
* Differences in pain concepts are individualized
* Name of muscles that are close to the prime mover but do not assist or are antagonist to the ROM focus
* Lack of understanding of expected findings related to specific pathology findings

Step 7. Use the previous information and write the distracters
~ Trapezius

~ Acute injuries can be manipulated if pain scale is under 4

~ Injury can be worked within 24 hours even with inflammation and spasms present

Step 8. Complete the item using the stem, key, and distracters.

The Massage Therapist must be mindful of the client and the client's pain tolerance. Ask more history questions to have a better understanding of the injury stage.

1. ROM helps to find out the muscles involved in the primary area and the compensating or pain posture offenders (**Key**).

2. Ask questions to see if the spasms are protecting the injury to determine if the client needs to see a doctor or if you are able to relieve the spasms.

3. Obtain information about what the client is wanting to achieve from this massage and give realistic information about your abilities, what you can and can't do, and why.

4. Create a treatment plan for the massage and give useful homework to obtain more relief.

In this example you can see that the question is asked at the Evaluation level of Bloom's Taxonomy. That is the highest form of question. It requires you to know information about each answer option, and then weigh each answer against the other to determine techniques and application.

In this sample question you can see that a client can still obtain a massage if acute injury protocol is followed. The right information must first be obtained within the assessment in order to apply helpful techniques. The MBLEx likes to make sure the client's safety comes first. It requires you to really think about each option and only use the information presented in the question and answers.

Massage-Exam.com would encourage every person to read all the available information on the MBLEx website. They detail for you how their tests are constructed and administered. Knowing this information helps you better prepare and be more confident in your ability to test.

Question 1: _____ is the study of the functions of an organism?

a. Pathophysiology
b. Physiology
c. Anatomy
d. None of the above

Question 2: A person in the _____ position is lying face up?

a. Prone
b. Supine
c. Recumbent
d. Ventral

Question 3: Choose from the following the definition of profession?

a. An occupation requiring training and specialized study
b. Skilled touch delivered to achieve a specific outcome with the recipient reimbursing for services rendered
c. A group of interacting elements that function as a complex whole
d. Replicating structures or functions that intertwine and influence each other

Question 4: Rotation of the head occurs because of this type of joint between the axis and atlas of the cervical vertebrae?

a. Hinge
b. Ellipsoid
c. Saddle
d. Pivot

Question 5: The two joints which create inversion and eversion are:

a. Proximal radioulnar and distal radioulnar
b. Metacarpophalangeal and Talocalcaneal
c. Talocrural and talocalcaneal
d. Talocalcaneal (subtalar) and talocalcaneonavicular

Question 6: So that therapists can develop a safe and effective treatment plan, it is necessary to have which of the following?

a. Receive payment before massage
b. Get a complete assessment of client's past and current health history
c. Include a disclaimer posted on your wall
d. All of the above

Question 7: The O in the acronym SOAP stands for?

a. Objective
b. Outline
c. Occurrence
d. Outsource

Question 8: To be able to have proper access to the supraspinatus tendon, which positioning would work best?

a. Internally rotating, extending, and ADducting the humerus
b. Externally rotating, extending, and ADducting the humerus
c. Internally rotating, flexing, and ADducting the humerus
d. Externally rotating, flexing, and ADducting the humerus

Question 9: A cramp is a:

a. Prolonged muscle spasm
b. Voluntary, prolonged muscle contraction
c. Involuntary, sustained contraction of a muscle
d. Short, painless, protective contraction

Question 10: What is the correct order of muscle layers, from superficial to deep, between the thoracic vertebrae and the medial border of the scapula?

a. Trapezius, ESGs, and rhomboids
b. Rhomboids, trapezius, and ESGs
c. Rhomboids, ESGs, and trapezius
d. Trapezius, rhomboids, and ESGs

Question 11: What muscle would be affected if the area of the superior angle on the scapula was tender to the touch?

a. Sternocleidomastoid
b. Scalenes
c. Trapezius
d. Levator scapula

Question 12: Out of all the muscles that attach to the humeroulnar and humeroradial joints, what muscle would be assessed when flexion is performed?

a. Triceps brachii
b. Ancones
c. Palmaris longus
d. All of the above

Question 13: Each state has varying regulations, which of the following is the best overall definition of scope of practice?

a. A group of interacting elements that function as a complex whole
b. A collection of tactile sensations that arise from sensory stimulation for the skin and deeper structures of the body
c. The knowledge base and practice parameters of a profession
d. The adherence to professional status, methods, standards, and character

Question 14: What bilateral action does the scalenes group perform?

a. Elevate ribs during inhalation
b. Depress ribs during expiration
c. Rotate head to the opposite side
d. Laterally flex the head and neck same side

Question 15: For the effectiveness of the massage, a comfortable balance of communication from both the client and the therapist is:

a. Up to the therapist
b. Ideal for treatment
c. Determined by client
d. Covered on the intake form

Question 16: Hypermobility is a joint dysfunction and defined as:

a. A disorder of the muscles of mastication and associated structures
b. A degeneration of the annular fibers of the intervertebral disc
c. A loss of motion and normal joint play movement at the joint
d. An increased degree of motion at the joint

Question 17: Which muscle ADducts the arm?

a. Biceps brachii
b. Latissimus dorsi
c. Supraspinatus
d. Rhomboid major

Question 18: The linea aspera is on the _____ aspect of the femur?

a. Posterior
b. Anterior
c. Lateral
d. Ipsilateral

Question 19: Which ribs are termed the floating ribs?

a. 8-12
b. 11 & 12
c. 10-12
d. 9-12

Question 20: The deltopectoral triangle sites of caution consist of:

a. Cephalic vein, clavicular artery, and pectoral nerve
b. Cephalic vein and thyroid gland
c. Superficial temporal artery and facial nerve
d. Hyoid bone, thyroid gland, and pectoral nerve

Question 21: What is the name of the two brothers who introduced Swedish Massage to the United States in 1856?

a. Dr. Charles Fayette Taylor and Dr. George Henry Taylor
b. Jacobi and Victoria A. White
c. Ambrose Pare and Per Henrik Ling
d. Dr. Johann Mezger and John Harvey Kellogg

Question 22: Tendons are a fibrous tissue that connect:

a. Muscle to bone
b. Bone to bone
c. Muscle to muscle
d. None of the above

Question 23: As a person exhales, the diaphragm will?

a. Expand and create a negative pressure drawing air into the lungs
b. Depress and create a positive pressure drawing air into the lungs
c. Contract and create a negative pressure drawing air into the lungs
d. Relaxes and creates a positive pressure drawing air out the lungs

Question 24: What is a definition of a dual or multidimensional relationship?

a. A professional relationship with a client who uses their insurance coverage to pay for the massage
b. A professional relationship between a massage therapist and another healthcare provider
c. A relationship that includes a complex and interwoven connection between a massage therapist and another person
d. A professional relationship between a business associate that provides services to a massage therapist

Question 25: What body system maintains posture, produces body heat, and movement?

a. Circulatory
b. Muscular
c. Gastrointestinal
d. Nervous

Question 26: To integrate your entire body within your manual manipulations utilizing all your tools, it is best to?

a. Use a variety of movements
b. Use the bodies weight
c. Use proper alignment
d. All of the above

Question 27: The hamstring muscles from lateral to medial are?

a. Biceps femoris, semitendenosus, and semimembranosus
b. Biceps femoris, semimembranosus, and semitendenosus
c. Semimembranosus, semitendenosus, and biceps femoris
d. Semitendenosus, semimembranosus, and biceps femoris

Question 28: Hyper/hypomobility, TMJD, degenerative disc disease and osteoarthritis are all?

a. Overuse injuries
b. Joint dysfunctions
c. Musculoskeletal injuries
d. Postural dysfunctions

Question 29: The main function of the spring ligament is to support the head of which bone?

a. Talus
b. Fibula
c. Tibia
d. Humerus

Question 30: When trying to determine if your client is in the acute or chronic stage of inflammation, when would pain manifest to the affected area?

a. Acute pain is aggravated by specific activity chronic is activated by activity and when at rest
b. Acute pain is constant and chronic has no pain
c. Acute pain is aggravated by activity and when at rest and chronic is only with specific activity
d. Acute pain has a decrease in the morning, and chronic is without pain in the morning

Question 31: The _____ is a strong plantarflexor and crosses both the knee and the ankle joints?

a. Tibialis anterior
b. Fibularis (peroneus) longus
c. Soleus
d. Gastrocnemius

Question 32: What is the purpose of a treatment description?

a. Create informed health care consumers
b. Create rapport
c. Create trust
d. All of the above

Question 33: The muscle spindles are proprioceptive nerve receptors or minute sensory organs located in the:

a. Muscle belly
b. Tendons
c. Joints
d. Capillaries

Question 34: Which of the following causes of wounds is a thermal force?

a. Chemical
b. Trauma
c. Pressure
d. Friction

Question 35: Of the following effects of hydrotherapy which is not an effect of a heat application?

a. Decrease circulation
b. Increase metabolism
c. Decrease pain
d. Decrease tissue stiffness

Question 36: The use of radiography to detect spinal subluxations and misalignment is within which scope of practice?

a. Podiatric Medicine
b. Chiropractic
c. Athletic Training
d. Psychology

Question 37: _____ is the study of the structure of organisms?

a. Anatomy
b. Physiology
c. Pathophysiology
d. None of the above

Question 38: What regulates the body temperature and is known as the thermostat of the body?

a. Skin
b. Liver
c. Hypothalamus
d. Cerebral cortex

Question 39: What muscle is palpable at the lateral cervical vertebrae and deep to the upper trapezius and is capable of moving the scapula?

a. Splenius capitis
b. Levator scapula
c. Scalenes
d. Rhomboid major

Question 40: What is the best way to access the rhomboid muscles while your client is in the prone position?

a. Both arms off the superior edge of the table
b. With their hand in the small of his back
c. With arm at a 90 degree angle off the table
d. The arm is placed right next to their side

Question 41: To palpate the posterior fibers of the scalenes, what muscles must you go between?

a. Levator scapula and middle scalenes
b. Longus capitis and middle scalenes
c. Splenius capitis and middle scalenes
d. SCM and middle scalenes

Question 42: Chronic bronchitis results in the production of purulent sputum and is termed a(n):

a. Condition of the CNS
b. Condition of the PNS
c. Circulatory pathology
d. Respiratory pathology

Question 43: Carpal tunnel syndrome (CTS) is a peripheral nervous system condition and is defined as a(n):

a. Condition that results from a compression of the median nerve
b. Condition that involves compression of the brachial plexus
c. Compression of the nerve as it passes through the anterior and middle scalenes
d. Compression of the nerve as it passes through the coracoid process and pectoralis minor

Question 44: Which of the following pathologies is not a musculoskeletal injury?

a. Strain/sprain
b. Fracture
c. Wounds and burns
d. Pes planus

Question 45: The muscle approximation technique uses the reflex effect of these cells to reduce tone or spasm in a muscle?

a. Golgi tendon
b. Mitochondria
c. Muscle spindle
d. Memory

Question 46: What are considered the main supportive components of the nervous system?

a. Fotons
b. Neurons
c. Protons
d. Axons

Question 47: The P in the acronym SOAP stands for?

a. Passive
b. Palpate
c. Project
d. Plan

Question 48: The Deltoid muscle has groups of fibers that perform different actions; the anterior fibers flex, medially rotate, and horizontally ADduct the glenohumeral joint. The posterior fibers extend, laterally rotate, and horizontally ABduct the glenohumeral joint. What is the one action that all the fibers (anterior, middle, and posterior) are in charge of?

a. ABduction of the glenohumeral joint
b. ADduction of the glenohumeral joint
c. Elevate the scapulothoracic joint

d. Depress the scapulothoracic joint

Question 49: Consent to treat is:

a. Not required for the client's insurance
b. Required to be filled out each massage
c. Required by law for therapists regulated under the health care act
d. Not required unless you feel it is necessary

Question 50: The endocrine system contains?

a. Pituitary, adrenal, and thyroid glands
b. Lymph nodes and lymph vessels
c. Skin, hair, and sweat glands
d. Gonads and genitals

Question 51: In order to locate the insertion site for the temporalis, what is the best action to have your client perform?

a. Open your mouth
b. Rotate your jaw from side to side
c. Clench and relax your jaw
d. All of the above

Question 52: Asthma is a respiratory pathology that is defined as a(n):

a. Chronic inflammatory disorder with bronchospasms
b. Condition that results in the production of purulent sputum
c. Enlargement of the air spaces distal to the terminal bronchioles and the destruction of the alveolar walls
d. Acute or chronic inflammation of the paranasal sinuses

Question 53: To treat trigger points and check for fascial restrictions with Petrissage, what type would be used as an assessment technique?

a. Light effleurage
b. Skin rolling
c. Lymphatic drainage
d. Vibration

Question 54: Osteoarthritis is a joint dysfunction and is defined as:

a. An increased degree of motion at the joint
b. A loss of motion and normal joint play movement at the joint
c. A degeneration of the annular fibers of the intervertebral disc
d. A group of chronic, degenerative conditions that affect the articular cartilage and subchondral bone of joints

Question 55: A new client intake reports they are diabetic, what treatments are contraindicated for this condition?

a. Petrissage and manual lymphatic drainage
b. Extreme hydrotherapy and deep cross-fiber friction
c. Petrissage and tapotement
d. Effleurage and petrissage

Question 56: What muscle extends the arm?

a. Coracobrachialis
b. Subclavius
c. Subscapularis
d. Teres major

Question 57: The muscle's reaction to dysfunction can be categorized into two groups; primarily postural and primarily phasic, which of the following is primarily a postural muscle?

a. Gastrocnemius
b. Peroneals
c. Tibialis anterior
d. Vastus lateralis

Question 58: How many curvatures are there in the spine?

a. 3
b. 5
c. 4
d. 2

Question 59: In order to palpate the contraction of serratus anterior using resistive techniques with your client in supine position, what position should the arm be in?

a. Anatomical position
b. Flexed shoulder with the fist raised to the ceiling
c. Flexed elbow tucked into their side
d. Arms at their side with hands curled into a fist

Question 60: Which of the following occupations is the study of athletic performance, injury prevention, and rehabilitation?

a. Osteopathic Medicine
b. Massage Therapy
c. Physical Therapy
d. Athletic Training

Question 61: A _____ is an overlapping alliance that a client and therapist share in addition to the therapeutic relationship.

a. Scope of Practice
b. Dual or Multidimensional relationship
c. Transference
d. Counter-Transference

Question 62: The cause of Ankylosing spondylitis is idiopathic and defined as:

a. An increase in the normal thoracic curve accompanied by protracted scapulae and head-forward posture
b. A chronic, systemic inflammatory disorder involving specific areas of the body, primarily the spine
c. A lateral rotatory deviation of the spine
d. An increase in normal lumbar curve and an increase in anterior pelvic tilt/ shortened hip flexors

Question 63: The muscle that performs opposite actions of the prime mover is an:

a. Synergist
b. Agonist
c. Aggressor
d. Antagonist

Question 64: To protect your radiocarpal joint when giving a massage, it is best to:

a. Keep your radiocarpal joint in radial deviation (ABduction)
b. Keep your radiocarpal joint in a neutral position
c. Keep your radiocarpal joint in ulnar deviation (ADduction)
d. Keep your radiocarpal joint in flexion

Question 65: Hydrotherapy is a form of complementary therapy that combines well with massage, one therapeutic use is analgesic which means a(n):

a. Reduction in sensation
b. Pain relief
c. Reduction in swelling
d. Reduction in fever

Question 66: Of the following choices, what would be a mechanical force causing a wound?

a. Extreme temperature
b. Chemical source
c. Trauma
d. Electrical source

Question 67: Which muscle group is located between the SCM and anterior flap of the Trapezius and unilaterally rotates the head and neck to the opposite side?

a. Splenius Capitis
b. Subclavius
c. Scalenes
d. Longissimus Capitis

Question 68: You work in the city and just instructed a co-worker to call 911 while beginning CPR on your unconscious boss, how long do you continue CPR?

a. After two 30/2 cycles
b. When you get tired
c. After five 15/2 cycles
d. A doctor or paramedic tells you to stop or takes over

Question 69: Which plane divides the body into right and left halves?

a. Frontal
b. Sagittal
c. Midsagittal
d. Transverse

Question 70: What is Transference?

a. A biological time machine into childhood emotions
b. Referring a client to another healthcare therapist
c. The nerve conduction from the spinal column to the peripheral limbs
d. Applying your own current feelings, emotions, or motivations onto another person

Question 71: When communicating with a client, care is taken not to lead the client or make assumptions about symptoms. What kind of questions are asked to assess the client's conditions?

a. Closed-ended
b. Leading
c. Assumed
d. Open-ended

Question 72: Which plane divides the body into an upper and a lower portion?

a. Frontal
b. Sagittal
c. Midsagittal
d. Transverse

Question 73: If you were talking about the integumentary system, you would be discussing?

a. The kidneys, lungs, pancreas, and spleen
b. The skin, nails, hair and sweat glands
c. The path that oxygen takes to bond with hemoglobin
d. The organs responsible for metabolism

Question 74: Keeping your hands clean is one of the best ways to prevent the spread of infection and illness in your practice. When is the best time to wash your hands?

a. Before and after a massage
b. Before a massage
c. After a massage
d. Just using hand sanitizer all the time is sufficient

Question 75: Which technique is specifically intended to disrupt and break down existing and forming adhesions in muscles, tendons, and ligaments?

a. GTO
b. Cross-fiber friction
c. Muscle approximation
d. Craniosacral therapy

Question 76: How many Kilocalories does each gram of fat produce?

a. Nine
b. Two
c. Four
d. Twenty

Question 77: Palpation is always performed _____, starting with the unaffected side.

a. Unilaterally
b. Ipsilaterally
c. Bilaterally
d. Medially

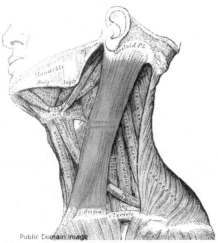

Public Domain Image

Question 78: The superficial SCM or sternocleidomastoid is on the lateral anterior aspect of the neck. At its origin it has two heads a sternal and clavicular, and the insertion is the mastoid process and lateral portion of the superior nuchal line on the occiput. Unilaterally it has two actions, bilaterally one. What is the bilateral action of the SCM?

a. Extend the head
b. Flex the head
c. Lateral flexion of head and neck to the same side
d. Rotation of head and neck to the opposite side

Question 79: The glenohumeral joint is freely movable and is functionaly classified as:

a. Synarthrotic
b. Fibrous
c. Diarthrotic
d. Cartilaginous

Question 80: In order to palpate the SITS rotator cuff muscle insertion sites, you must place your thumb and fingers where?

a. Thumb on the lesser tubercle and 2nd-4th finger tips on the greater tubercle
b. Thumb on the greater tubercle and 2nd-4th finger tips on the lesser tubercle
c. Thumb on the acromion process and 2nd-4th finger tips on the greater tubercle
d. Thumb on the coracoid process and 2nd-4th finger tips on the greater tubercle

Question 81: What is the most common cause of death among those who have experienced a burn?

a. Periostitis
b. Sepsis
c. Compartment syndromes
d. Hyperkyphosis

Question 82: In a ninth century temple carving in India, who can be found getting a massage?

a. Ambroise Pare
b. Buddha
c. Galen of Rome
d. Yellow Emperor

Question 83: The _____ _____ divides the body into left and right portions.

a. Transverse plane
b. Mid-sagittal plane
c. Frontal plane
d. Sagittal plane

Question 84: When a body is divided into anterior and posterior portions, it is called the:

a. Sagittal plane
b. Frontal plane
c. Transverse plane
d. Mid-sagittal plane

Question 85: What action can you have your client perform to distinguish between the posterior scalene and levator scapula?

a. Rotate your head back and forth
b. Take a deep breath
c. Slowly bring your shoulder up toward your ear
d. Slowly bring your ear down toward your shoulder

Question 86: A summary or outline of standards to which a Massage Therapist agrees to conduct their massage practices with a declaration of acceptable, ethical, and general principles of professional behavior is the _____.

a. Standards of Practice
b. Code of Ethics
c. Code of Policies
d. Standard of Regulations

Question 87: You are assessing your clients thumb and find that there is pain on extension and ABduction, what muscle is indicated?

a. Extensor pollicis longus
b. Extensor pollicis brevis
c. ABductor pollicis longus
d. ABductor pollicis brevis

Question 88: To properly treat the SCM on a client with left-sided torticollis you can utilize isometric agonist contraction techniques on what directional planes?

a. Lateral flexion and rotation
b. Flexion and extension
c. Flexion and rotation
d. Lateral flexion and extension

Question 89: Generally, any technique applied in a slow, rhythmical, and repetitive manner will evoke a relaxation response and _____.

a. Increase sympathetic nervous system firing
b. Decrease parasympathetic nervous system firing
c. Increase both the sympathetic and parasympathetic firing
d. Decrease sympathetic nervous system firing

Question 90: _____ is the displacement or transfer of latent emotions, thoughts, feelings, and behaviors originally related to childhood experiences that can be triggered by treatment work.

a. Transference
b. Boundary
c. Competency
d. Counter-Transference

Question 91: To reduce symptoms, some massage treatments can be temporarily uncomfortable, such as friction. It is best to:

a. Work within the clients pain tolerance
b. Work through treatment knowing that the treatment is painful, but for the best
c. Have the client focus to help with pain
d. Use plenty of lotion

Question 92: If you cut your finger or have an open hangnail you must use a _____ during the massage.

a. Reusable glove
b. Band-Aid
c. Finger cot
d. Gauze strip

Question 93: Who is given credit for the invention of Swedish Massage?

a. Galen of Rome
b. Yellow Emperor
c. Per Henrik Ling
d. Buddha

Question 94: Which muscle has its insertion at a groove on the clavicle?

a. Pectoralis major
b. Pectoralis minor
c. Sternocleidomastoid
d. Subclavius

Question 95: What body system is in charge of maintaining homeostasis, reproduction, and metabolism?

a. Nervous
b. Endocrine
c. Circulatory
d. Lymphatic

Question 96: A slightly movable joint is known as:

a. Amphiarthrotic
b. Diarthrotic
c. Synarthrotic
d. Synovial

Question 97: When scheduling your client for their next massage, it is better to:

a. Show them your schedule and have them pick the best time
b. Ask for their day and time preference
c. Schedule them when you have a spot and they can call to change if there is a problem
d. Automatically have them on the same day and same time, billing the insurance even if they don't come

Question 98: Adhesive capsulitis is another name for which pathology?

a. Pes Planus
b. TMJD
c. Degenerative Disc Disease
d. Frozen shoulder

Question 99: When performing a client assessment before treatments, an effective therapist will?

a. Balance the neutral caring approach and the technical investigative approach
b. Push the client past their pain tolerance to determine which muscles are involved
c. Forgo the assessments because it might cause pain
d. Utilize a gait assessment which is enough to determine your treatment plan

Question 100: If your client has a moderate anterior pelvic tilt what three muscles would be shortened?

a. Iliacus, psoas major and rectus femoris
b. Biceps femoris, gluteus maximus and semitendinosus
c. Biceps femoris, sartorius and gluteus medius
d. Adductor magnus, gluteus maximus and gluteus medius

Question 101: Any repeated activity, occupational or recreational, can lead to an/a:

a. Postural dysfunction
b. Joint dysfunction
c. Musculoskeletal injury
d. Overuse injury

Question 102: Which muscle is also commonly called the "boxer's muscle"?

a. Serratus anterior
b. Trapezius
c. Triceps Brachii
d. Biceps brachii

Question 103: The cranial sutures are structurally fibrous with no defined movement, what is their functional classification?

a. Synarthrotic
b. Amphiarthrotic
c. Cartilaginous
d. Diarthrotic

Question 104: Postural dysfunctions have two classifications, what are they?

a. Functional and dysfunctional
b. Dysfunctional and structural
c. Structural and functional
d. Structural and connected

Question 105: Lymphatic drainage technique reduces:

a. Lymph flow
b. Capillary flow
c. Node refill
d. Edema and pain

Question 106: Situated between the posterior scalenes and the splenius capitus is what muscle?

a. Middle scalenes
b. Levator scapula
c. ESGs
d. Trapezius

Question 107: When treating clients who are pregnant or have cardiovascular concerns, it is important to know:

a. If they have had surgery
b. What they do for work
c. The client's blood pressure
d. None of the above

Question 108: Linda is an IT manager who has been noticing that her team complaints about body pain have been increasing. They have upgraded all the workstations ergonomically, hoping that would take care of the issues. She wants to know if there is a type of massage that could help. Linda would also like her team to be educated on proper posture and alignment in repetitive movements. What modality can you refer her to?

a. Aston-Patterning
b. Aromatherapy
c. Equine Massage
d. Attunement Therapy

Question 109: The resistance of a relaxed muscle to passively stretch or elongate is described as:

a. Muscle approximation
b. Muscle tone
c. Muscle strength
d. Muscle weakness

Question 110: An example of a long bone would be?

a. The sternum
b. The humerus
c. A rib
d. Cranium

Question 111: If you were to start at the anterior flap of the upper trapezius and move anteriorly, what order would you palpate the following muscles?

a. Trapezius, posterior scalene, levator scapula, middle and anterior scalenes
b. Trapezius, levator scapula, posterior, middle and anterior scalenes
c. Trapezius, splenii, posterior, middle and anterior scalenes
d. Trapezius, longus capitis, anterior, middle and posterior scalenes

Question 112: What two unilateral actions are the scalenes in charge of?

a. Rotation to the same side and lateral flexion to the opposite side
b. Rotation to the opposite side and lateral flexion to the same side
c. Flexion and rotation to the same side
d. Elevation of the ribs in inhalation and rotation to the opposite side

Question 113: What technique is used to reduce edema, ease pain, lower the chance of scar tissue formation, and remove metabolic waste secondary to edema and inflammation?

a. Muscle approximation
b. Lymphatic drainage
c. Diaphragmatic breathing
d. Pressure point

Question 114: If the body is in Homeostasis, it means that the?

a. Organ systems will eventually fail
b. Systems of the body are working too hard to sustain life
c. Body is in a state of equilibrium
d. Seizure is over

Question 115: The autonomic nervous system (ANS) controls?

a. Voluntary functions
b. Skeletal muscle movements
c. Brain and spinal cord functions
d. Glands, cardiac, and smooth muscle

Question 116: All information given is confidential on a health history intake form unless?

a. The client gives specific written permission
b. Their HCP asks for it
c. You feel it is your duty to share client information for legal reasons
d. Treatments are complete and they are no longer a client

Question 117: The A in the acronym SOAP stands for?

a. Application
b. Assessment
c. Agreement
d. Access

Question 118: Relative to its size, this muscle is the strongest muscle in the body, it can manage nearly one hundred-fifty pounds of pressure.

a. Anterior Scalene
b. Medial Pterygoid
c. Teres Minor
d. Masseter

Question 119: With a muscle injury, active free and passive relaxed range of motion are used to assess:

a. Synergists
b. Pain in the muscle's range
c. The client's tolerance to compressed pain
d. Where the trigger points are effecting the muscles

Question 120: The _____ ligament is composed of several ligaments that originate at the medial malleolus. It is designed to protect against medial stress of the talocrural joint?

a. Spring
b. Deltoid
c. Long plantar
d. Lateral talocalcaneal

Question 121: The S in the acronym SOAP stands for?

a. Stand
b. Succeed
c. Subjective
d. Source

Question 122: For better exposure of the scalenes, how can you position the head?

a. Lateral flexion to the same side
b. Lateral flexion to the opposite side
c. Rotate head to the same side
d. Rotate head slightly to the opposite side

Question 123: The massage profession has many methods that are popular, which of the following is a neuromuscular approach?

a. Reflexology
b. Touch of health
c. Three-in-one concepts
d. Educational kinesiology

Question 124: Your client suffers from hyperglycemia, this is a result of:

a. Low blood oxidation levels
b. High blood oxidation levels
c. Low blood glucose levels
d. High blood glucose levels

Question 125: What are the 3 types of muscles in the human body?

a. Nerve, epithelial, and skeletal
b. Skeletal, cardiac, and smooth
c. Long, short, and cardiac
d. Visceral, skeletal, and epithelial

Question 126: _____ muscle is not under our conscious control and is termed involuntary?

a. Striated
b. Skeletal
c. Smooth
d. None of the above

Question 127: Which of the following forms would you file with the IRS if you had a contract with another company and was paid over $600 for your services?

a. W-9
b. 1099-Misc
c. 1040
d. 1040EZ

Question 128: The Standard of Practice in regards to Confidentiality is in respect to:

a. All client information
b. Sexual misconduct
c. All business practices
d. Dual or multidimensional relationships

Question 129: What forearm muscle would be assessed when both pronation and supination are performed?

a. Biceps brachii
b. Brachioradialis
c. Pronator teres
d. Supinator

Question 130: When using your CPR/ First aid skills on a suspected stroke victim, you must think:

a. 30 compressions and 2 breaths
b. ABCs
c. R.I.C.E
d. F.A.S.T.

Question 131: All of the following muscles share the same attachment site:

a. Pectoralis minor, Biceps brachii, and Brachialis
b. Biceps brachii, Coracobrachialis, and Pectoralis minor
c. Brachialis, Coracobrachialis, and Biceps brachii
d. Coracobrachialis, Pectoralis minor, and Brachialis

Question 132: As the tissue heals from a wound or burn, modifications of hydrotherapy treatments are required when applying to the affected area because of:

a. Pressure
b. Hypersensitivity to temperature extremes
c. Scar tissue
d. Disruption of continuity of the skin

Question 133: What are the three phases in acute inflammation?

a. 1: Change in vascular flow, 2: change in vascular permeability and 3: cellular events
b. 1: Vasoconstriction, 2: decrease in lymphatic fluid and 3: cellular events
c. 1: Decreased permeability, 2: decreased blood flow and 3: decreased WBCs
d. 1: Diaphedesis, 2: chemotaxis and 3: phagocytosis

Question 134: Scoliosis is a postural dysfunction and is defined as:

a. A lateral rotatory deviation of the spine
b. An increase in the normal thoracic curve accompanied by protracted scapulae and head-forward posture
c. An increase in normal lumbar curve and an increase in anterior pelvic tilt/ shortened hip flexors
d. A chronic, systemic inflammatory disorder involving specific areas of the body, primarily the spine

Question 135: _____ is also known as the master gland?

a. The thyroid gland
b. The pituitary gland
c. The parathyroid gland
d. The adrenal glands

Question 136: The best way to locate the intertubercular groove that houses the biceps brachii tendon, is to:

a. Medially rotate the arm
b. Flex the arm
c. Extend the arm
d. Laterally rotate the arm

Question 137: If an assessment or diagnosis has already been made for your client it is best to:

a. Ask for copies of transcripts and treat on that information alone
b. Achieve your own understanding of the clients' condition
c. Perform massage without testing conditions
d. Go with the recommended treatments without gathering any further information

Question 138: What structures would be shortened with a chronic varus stress of the tibiofemoral joint?

a. Biceps femoris and IT band
b. Vastus lateralis and tensor fasciae latae
c. Semimembranosus, semitendinosus and gracilis
d. Tensor fasciae latae and IT band

Question 139: The major components of the nervous system are?

a. Branch nerves and trunk nerves
b. The spinal cord and brain
c. The nerves
d. The peripheral nervous system

Question 140: Which of the following pathologies is not a condition of the Peripheral Nervous System?

a. Spinal cord injury
b. Radial nerve lesions
c. Ulnar nerve lesions
d. Median nerve lesions

Question 141: If your client is suffering from chronic valgus stress, what ligament might be damaged?

a. Lateral collateral ligament
b. Medial collateral ligament
c. Anterior cruciate ligament
d. Posterior cruciate ligament

Question 142: What type of joint movement would you use to describe the act of bringing a limb in towards the midline of the body?

a. ABduction
b. ADduction
c. Flexion
d. Extension

Question 143: _____ is a declaration of the general principles of acceptable, ethical, and professional behavior by which massage therapists agree to conduct their practice?

a. Code of ethics
b. Scope of practice
c. Client confidentiality law
d. Review of client's health history

Question 144: An Iliotibial band contracture is defined as:

a. Inflammation and pain at the lateral femoral condyle and IT band juncture
b. A painful degenerative change to the articular cartilage on the underside of the patella
c. A decrease in the medial longitudinal arch and a pronated hindfoot
d. A contracture or thickening of the IT band

Question 145: Which muscle of the leg is involved in the flexion of the thigh?

a. Pectineus
b. Iliopsoas
c. Tensor fascia latae
d. All of the above

Question 146: What system in the body regulates and maintains tissue fluids and combats disease?

a. Immune System
b. Lymphatic
c. Circulatory
d. Urinary

Question 147: To keep your back safe from discomfort or injury while in a massage, you must?

a. Bend at the spine
b. Bend at the hip joints
c. Increase the Kyphotic curve
d. Increase Lordotic curve

Question 148: To bring the coracoacromial ligament closer to the surface, what action will roll the humeral head anteriorly, pressing the ligament forward?

a. Flexion
b. ADduction
c. Extension
d. ABduction

Question 149: What type of ROM testing is used to pinpoint adhesions?

a. Adson's
b. Babinski's
c. Active resisted
d. Bragard's sign

Question 150: What three landmarks do you palpate between to find the muscle belly of the deltoid?

a. Acromion, medial 1/3 of the clavicle and deltoid tuberosity
b. Coracoid process, lateral 1/3 of the clavicle and deltoid tubercle
c. Acromion, medial 1/3 of the clavicle and deltoid tubercle
d. Acromion, lateral 1/3 of the clavicle and deltoid tuberosity

Question 151: A(n) _____ muscle has the opposite desired action of a _____ muscle.

a. Agonistic/antagonist
b. Antagonist/agonist
c. Prime mover/antagonist
d. Prime mover/agonist

Question 152: Most long nerve fibers are covered with a whitish, fatty material that is called:

a. Nissel
b. Dendrites
c. Myelin
d. Synapse

Question 153: What body system produces blood cells and stores minerals?

a. Lymphatic
b. Circulatory
c. Skeletal
d. Muscular

Question 154: What does ABC stand for in first aid/ CPR, when checking an unconscious person?

a. Airway, Breathing, and Cardiac
b. Align, Breathing, and Cardiac
c. Airway, Breathing, and Circulation
d. Airway, Bleeding, and Circulation

Question 155: If a client has a subluxation, you would refer them to a:

a. Nutritionist
b. Chiropractor
c. Acupuncturist
d. Podiatrist

Question 156: The endocrine system _____.

a. Involves the fingernails and skin
b. Is responsible for hemoglobin transport
c. Is a rarely used system in the autonomic structure
d. Produces hormones and secretes them into the blood

Question 157: When applying deep pressure using your olecranon process or elbow, you must:

a. Use your free hand to palpate and guide it
b. Use the other elbow at the same time
c. Keep your fist tense at all times
d. None of the above

Question 158: Which of the following choices is part of the endocrine system?

a. Pancreas, thyroid, and bile
b. Thyroid, pharynx, and adrenal
c. Adrenal, gonads, and thyroid
d. Gonads, pharynx, and larynx

Question 159: What action is used to assess scapulohumeral rhythm at the scapula or scapulothoracic joint?

a. Downward rotation
b. Upward rotation
c. ADduction
d. ABduction

Question 160: What is the definition of contraindication?

a. A fungal infecton caused by yeast
b. A deep inflammatory condition affecting the superficial to subcutaneous skin
c. A superficial proliferation of blood vessels or telangiectasis
d. A symptom or circumstance that makes treatment inappropriate

Question 161: In postural dysfunctions, the slow twitch postural muscle group:

a. Fatigues fast
b. Fatigues slow
c. Never fatigues
d. None of the above

Question 162: What muscle is an ADductor of the arm?

a. Biceps brachii
b. Sternocleidomastoid
c. Coracobrachialis
d. Brachialis

Question 163: The _____ is the minimum standard adhered to by a therapist for safe and effective practice.

a. Impugn
b. Competency
c. Dual or Multidimensional relationship
d. Scope of Practice

Question 164: The treatment plan is something developed by the therapist with input from the:

a. Client
b. PA
c. ROM testing
d. All of the above

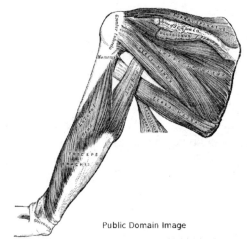

Public Domain Image

Question 165: The Triceps Brachii has one action on the elbow or humeroulnar joint and two actions on the glenohumeral or shoulder joint. What is the one action all three heads perform at the elbow?

a. Extension
b. Flexion
c. Lateral rotation
d. Medial rotation

Question 166: A client presents left-side torticollis, what muscle would be shortened and most effected?

a. Left pectoralis major
b. Right pectoralis major
c. Left SCM
d. Right SCM

Question 167: What does the Eustachian tube do?

a. Connects the uterus to uvula
b. Connects the ovary to the uterus
c. Connects the pancreas to bile duct
d. Connects the middle ear with the nasal cavity

Question 168: With your client prone and the arm at a 90 degree angle hanging off the side of the table, how do you find the muscle belly of the middle fibers of the trapezius?

a. By sliding laterally and superior from the lateral border of the scapula
b. By sliding medially and superior from the spine of the scapula
c. By sliding medially and inferior from the spine of the scapula
d. By sliding laterally and inferior from the spine of the scapula

Question 169: A person who is lying prone would be?

a. On the ventral surface of their body
b. On the dorsal surface of their body
c. On their side with knees drawn up
d. None of the above

Question 170: Degenerative disc disease is a joint dysfunction and defined as:

a. A degeneration of the annular fibers of the intervertebral disc
b. A loss of motion and normal joint play movement at the joint
c. An increased degree of motion at the joint
d. A disorder of the muscles of mastication and associated structures

Question 171: Leaving a client's health history document lying on the counter during a massage is:

a. Ok if you are not busy
b. Permitted if you are in a hurry
c. Breaching client confidentiality laws
d. Not something to be worried about

Question 172: Inaccuracies will occur in performing orthopedic testings if:

a. There is too much movement
b. It is repeated too many times
c. The clients concentration is broken
d. None of the above

Question 173: What are the two most popular stances among MT's?

a. The parallel and T stance
b. The parallel and one-foot forward stance
c. The one-foot forward and T stance
d. The T and Y stance

Question 174: Which muscle is responsible for head, neck, and shoulder movements?

a. Sternocleidomastoid
b. Levator scapulae
c. Scalenes
d. Trapezius

Question 175: What system of the body would help absorb nutrients?

a. Gastrointestinal
b. Circulatory
c. Lymphatic
d. Endocrine

Question 176: What is the best definition for Origin-Insertion Approximation?

a. A client actively shortens the muscle at the musculotendinous junction
b. A resisted contraction that shortens the muscle at the musculotendinous junction
c. A passive shortening of the muscle at the musculotendinous junction
d. A passive lengthening of the muscle at the musculotendinous junction

Question 177: How many pairs of nerves branch off of the spine?

a. 31
b. 36
c. 32
d. 26

Question 178: As a person inhales, the diaphragm will?

a. Expand and create a negative pressure drawing air into the lungs
b. Expand and create a positive pressure drawing air into the lungs
c. Contract and create a negative pressure drawing air into the lungs
d. Contract and create a positive pressure drawing air into the lungs

Question 179: Which of the following massage profession methods is an approach of applied kinesiology?

a. Zero balancing
b. Reiki
c. Polarity
d. Touch of health

Question 180: The "Yellow Emperor's Classics of Internal Medicine", China's oldest Medical book, contained massage treatments for:

a. Headaches
b. Neck pain
c. Shoulder pain
d. Paralysis and reduced circulation

Question 181: Which of the following body systems is in charge of muscular development?

a. Nervous system
b. Digestive system
c. Lymphatic system
d. Endocrine system

Question 182: Which of the following is not part of the upper respiratory system?

a. Larynx
b. Vocal cords
c. Mouth
d. Trachea

Question 183: Which muscle has its origin at the aponeurotic fibers of the iliolumbar ligament and the iliac crest?

a. Gracilis
b. Sartorius
c. Quadratus lumborum
d. Psoas major

Question 184: In anatomical position, which bone of the forearm is lateral?

a. Radius
b. Ulna
c. Humerus
d. Tibia

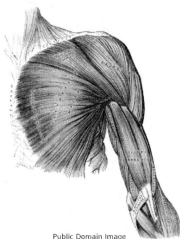

Public Domain Image

Question 185: The superficial pectoralis major is divided into three sections; clavicular, sternal, and costal fibers. This muscle also is an antagonist to itself with its upper and lower fibers. What are the actions of the upper fibers?

a. Extension and ADduction of the glenohumeral joint
b. Extension of the glenohumeral joint
c. Flexion and horizontal ABduction of the glenohumeral joint
d. Flexion and horizontal ADduction of the glenohumeral joint

Question 186: Decreasing muscle spasm and increasing the resting length of muscles is an effect of:

a. Mechanical stimulation of golgi tendon organs
b. Chemical stimulation of golgi tendon organs
c. Reflexive stimulation of golgi tendon organs
d. Mechanical stimulation of the muscle spindle cells

Question 187: The insertion of needles and the application of moxibustion is within which of the following occupation's scope of practice?

a. Psychology
b. Podiatric Medicine
c. Acupuncture
d. Athletic Training

Question 188: Which of the following muscles attach to the IT band?

a. Semitendenosus
b. Tensor fascia latae
c. Rectus femoris
d. Semimembranosus

Question 189: Of the following pathologies, what is not a respiratory condition?

a. Sinusitis
b. Emphysema
c. Hemiplegia
d. Asthma

Question 190: What is the main portion or the shaft of the bone called?

a. Compact bone
b. Bone marrow
c. Medullary cavity
d. Diaphysis

Question 191: The abdomen can be separated into four quadrants, which of the following is within the left lower quadrant (LLQ)?

a. Sigmoid colon and left ovary/ tube
b. Liver, gallbladder, duodenum, pancreas, right kidney, and hepatic flexure.
c. Stomach, spleen, left kidney, pancreas, and splenic flexure
d. Cecum, appendix, and right ovary/ tube

Question 192: Your client sits at a computer for more than 10 hours a day Monday through Friday, what five muscles of the hip and thigh are shortened?

a. Iliacus, psoas major, semitendinosus, semimembranosus and gluteus medius
b. Gluteus maximus, biceps femoris, semitendinosus, semimembranosus and gluteus medius
c. Iliacus, psoas major, rectus femoris, sartorius and gluteus medius
d. Iliacus, gluteus maximus, biceps femoris, sartorius and gluteus medius

Question 193: A lack of vitamin D, pain resulting from inflammation, and direct or indirect trauma of infection can cause:

a. Trigger Points
b. Muscle spasm and cramps
c. Prolonged eccentric contractions
d. Prolonged concentric contractions

Question 194: Branches of the brachial plexus and subclavian artery pass through what two muscles?

a. SCM and middle scalenes
b. Longus capitis and posterior scalenes
c. Splenius capitis and posterior scalenes
d. Anterior and middle scalenes

Question 195: What term is indicated when a client becomes emotional after meeting with their MT because their MT resembles a relative that has just passed away?

a. Reflexive
b. Transference
c. Professional
d. Dual relationship

Question 196: As a reaction to the presence of foreign particles, the body's immune system may create?

a. Antagonists
b. Antigens
c. Antibodies
d. Antagonons

Question 197: What two actions are most frequently restricted significantly and are painful in Frozen shoulder conditions?

a. ABduction and external rotation
b. ADduction and internal rotation
c. ABduction and internal rotation
d. ADduction and external rotation

Question 198: What is Projection?

a. A diagnosis given only by massage therapists
b. Applying your own current feelings, emotions, or motivations onto another person
c. A biological time machine into childhood emotions
d. A nerve impulse reaction stimulated by a spinal column manipulation

Question 199: Where can you find the temporal bone?

a. Elbow
b. Temperinium
c. Skull
d. Hand

Question 200: Brandon is a pitcher and has recently been given a diagnosis of carpal tunnel syndrome from his team doctor. He would like to do everything in his power to get rid of this pain so he can avoid surgery. He has two more years on his scholarship and would like to keep it. Massage has been helping with a reduction in his pain, but he still needs to improve before he can be given the green light to pitch again. He has taken a month off of training in the off-season and would like to know if there is anything additional he could be doing. What technique would you refer Brandon to in order to gain a better understanding of his posture and alignment to avoid surgery?

a. Acupressure
b. Active Isolated Stretching
c. Amma
d. Alexander Technique

Question 201: For treatment of a repeat client it is best to:

a. Check notes and repeat last treatment
b. Assume treatment is working with out communicating with client
c. Review the client's health history (HH)/SOAP's and request feedback on effects of the treatment
d. Change treatment plan every time

Question 202: What is the anatomical word for collar bone?

a. Calcaneus
b. Sternum
c. Scapula
d. Clavicle

Question 203: When assessing the radiocarpal joint, what muscle group would you lengthen to release or decrease mild extension at the wrist?

a. Extensors
b. Flexors
c. Radial deviators
d. Ulnar deviators

Question 204: The tibialis anterior and fibularis (peroneus) longus support the:

a. Frontal arch
b. Longitudinal arch
c. Transverse arch
d. Sagittal arch

Question 205: What bone in the body does not articulate with other bones?

a. Choroid
b. Hyoid
c. Patella
d. The floating ribs

Question 206: What is the best position to palpate the superior angle of the scapula?

a. Supine with arm flexed at 90 degrees
b. Sidelying with scapula inferiorly depressed towards the feet
c. Sidelying with scapula superiorly elevated towards the head
d. All of the above

Question 207: To breakdown adhesions that prevent normal motion, this technique can be used in sub-acute and chronic stages of healing?

a. Effleurage
b. Rhythmic mobilization
c. Myofascial release
d. Cross-fiber friction

Question 208: When using your thumb without reinforcements you must:

a. Keep your wrist and forearm bent
b. Use your other thumb as well
c. Keep it in line with the radius
d. Tense your wrist and forearm muscles

Question 209: What are the four "T"s of palpation?

a. Treatment, texture, tenderness, and tone
b. Temperature, tone, tenderness, and texture
c. Texture, tension, tenderness, and testing
d. Testing, tone, texture, and tenderness

Question 210: Which of the following body systems is in charge of regulating body temperature and transporting nutrients / hormones?

a. Lymphatic
b. Nervous
c. Circulatory
d. Endocrine

Question 211: A(n) _____ compression is a static compression applied by the therapist's thumbs, fingertips, or olecranon to a trigger point?

a. InNervation
b. Valvular
c. Intrinsic conduction
d. Ischemic

Question 212: _____ is the study and development of a particular skill or professional knowledge base associated and applied within a scope of practice.

a. Dual or Multidimensional relationship
b. Boundary
c. Competency
d. Transference

Question 213: Which one of the following would the parasympathetic nervous system control?

a. Elevating blood pressure
b. Fight or flight responses
c. Slowing down the heart; intestinal activity
d. All of the above

Question 214: What is the bony landmark on the humerus that houses the forearm flexors?

a. Greater tubercle
b. Lesser tubercle
c. Medial supracondylar ridge
d. Lateral supracondylar ridge

Question 215: Which system of the body would regulate the blood pH and exchange gases?

a. Circulatory
b. Gastrointestinal
c. Integumentary
d. Respiratory

Question 216: If a client comes to you with a headache that has referred pain, it is most likely a:

a. Cluster headache
b. Tension headache
c. Migraine
d. Chronic paroxysmal hemicrania

Question 217: While it is regrettable, transference does happen during treatments. If you encounter a client who has experienced a negative childhood emotion and transferred an irrational reaction towards you, it is best to:

a. Continue the massage as if nothing has happened and use effleurage only
b. Allow the client to be informed of the transference and possibility give them the option of ending the session or having a moment to themselves. Always respect the clients needs (within reason)
c. Terminate the session, communicating that you can't work with unstable emotions. It's not within your scope of practice
d. Communicate to them that these things happen and there is nothing that can be done except to end the session

Question 218: What two muscles ADduct the scapula?

a. Latissimus dorsi and rhomboids
b. Rhomboids and trapezius (middle fibers)
c. Rhomboids and latissimus dorsi
d. Latissimus dorsi and Trapezius

Question 219: Thoracic outlet syndrome (TOS) is a peripheral nervous system condition defined as a(n):

a. Progressively diminishing basal ganglia function
b. Condition where demyelination of the nerves occurs
c. Motor function disorder resulting from damage to the immature brain
d. Condition that involves compression of the brachial plexus

Question 220: Plantar fasciitis is an inflammation of the plantar fascia and termed an:

a. Overuse injury
b. Systemic condition
c. Joint dysfunction
d. Musculoskeletal injury

Question 221: Which of the following pathologies is not a condition of the Central Nervous System?

a. Seizures
b. Radial nerve lesions
c. Parkinsons
d. Cerebral palsy

Question 222: What body system detects sensations and controls movements?

a. Nervous
b. Integumentary
c. Muscular
d. Circulatory

Question 223: While your client is seated, what position should the arm be in to be able to feel the antagonistic abilities of the posterior and anterior deltoid fibers?

a. Arm at their side with elbow flexed
b. Arm ADducted
c. Arm horizontally medially rotated
d. Arm outstretched into flexion in front of the body

Question 224: Using your palm allows for a broader surface contact, which of the following positions is correct?

a. Maintain wrist joint and forearm alignment with fingers and thumb relaxed
b. Maintain ulnar deviation (ADduction) of the wrist with constant pressure
c. Maintain radial deviation (ABduction) or the wrist with light pressure
d. Maintain wrist joint and forearm alignment with fingers and thumb flexed

Question 225: Which of the two lower leg bones is the largest?

a. Ulna
b. Fibula
c. Femur
d. Tibia

Public Domain Image

Question 226: The Gluteus Medius has anterior and posterior fibers, what actions are the anterior fibers in charge of?

a. Extension and lateral rotation of the coxal joint
b. Flexion and medial rotation of the coxal joint
c. Flexion and lateral rotation of the coxal joint
d. Extension and medial rotation of the coxal joint

Question 227: Which of the following choices would the sympathetic nervous system control?

a. Pupillary responses
b. Constriction of blood vessels
c. Slowing down the heart; intestinal activity
d. Lowered respiratory rate

Question 228: Sebaceous glands are found in which layer of tissue?

a. Subcutaneous
b. Epidermis
c. Dermis
d. Pangaea

Question 229: Multiple sclerosis (MS) is a condition that causes demyelination of nerves, it is termed a:

a. Condition of the PNS
b. Condition of the CNS
c. Systemic concern
d. Musculoskeletal injury

Question 230: When a therapist files all applicable state and federal taxes, they are following the Standard of Practice under which section?

a. Confidentiality
b. Business Practices
c. Roles and Boundaries
d. Prevention of Sexual Misconduct

Question 231: Who can request health history information without written consent of the client?

a. Spouse
b. Physician
c. Anyone by Court Order
d. Son or daughter

Question 232: A spasm is:

a. A voluntary, prolonged muscle contraction
b. A short muscle contraction
c. An involuntary, sustained contraction of a muscle
d. A painful, voluntary, quick muscle contraction

Question 233: A functional postural dysfunctions:

a. Is due to altered bone shapes
b. Can be caused by malformations
c. Can be altered by working with the soft tissue and fascia
d. Cannot be corrected with massage

Question 234: Of the following choices, which is the best that defines professionalism?

a. An occupation requiring training and specialized study
b. A group of interacting elements that function as a complex whole
c. One who engages in a profession
d. The adherence to professional status, methods, standards, and character

Question 235: When you treat each client with dignity, respect, and worth, you are adhering to which Standard of Practice?

a. Roles and Boundaries
b. Professionalism
c. Legal and Ethical Requirements
d. Confidentiality

Question 236: Which system eliminates waste from the circulatory system and balances water within the body?

a. Nervous
b. Circulatory
c. Urinary
d. Lymphatic

Question 237: If your client has a moderate posterior pelvic tilt what three muscles would be lengthened?

a. Iliacus, psoas major and biceps femoris
b. Iliacus, psoas major and rectus femoris
c. Biceps femoris, gluteus maximus and semitendinosus
d. Gluteus maximus (all fibers), gluteus medius and ADductor magnus

Question 238: Piriformis syndrome is a peripheral nervous system condition and is defined as a(n):

a. Condition that involves compression of the brachial plexus
b. Compression of the sciatic nerve
c. Condition that results from a compression of the median nerve
d. Compression of the nerve as it passes through the anterior and middle scalenes

Question 239: You have performed a postural assessment on your client who was in a marathon three days ago, both legs have mild lateral rotation, what muscle would be short and hypertonic?

a. Gluteus minimus
b. TFL
c. Piriformis
d. Gracilis

Question 240: In the 1932 Dr. Emil and Estrid Vodder develop what technique?

a. Polarity Therapy
b. Manual Lymphatic Drainage
c. Connective tissue massage
d. Orthopedic Medicine

Question 241: To prevent infectious and communicable diseases the simplest, most effective way to minimize risk is hand washing. The CDC has four steps for proper hand washing. What is the fourth step?

a. Dry hands with a paper towel
b. Rub hands together for at least 20 seconds to work up a lather
c. Apply soap to hands
d. Rinse hands using warm water

Question 242: What muscle would you be assessing with a severe downward rotation of the scapulothoracic joint?

a. Trapezius (lower fibers)
b. Trapezius (upper fibers)
c. Levator scapula
d. Pectoralis minor

Question 243: The connective tissue within the medullary cavity is called?

a. Spongy bone
b. Bone marrow
c. Periosteum
d. Endosteum

Question 244: A _____ is a limit that is adhered to in order to separate and protect the integrity of all parties involved.

a. Competency
b. Transference
c. Boundary
d. Dual or Multidimensional relationship

Question 245: What system of the body removes waste from the circulatory system?

a. Urinary
b. Lymphatic
c. Nervous
d. Endocrine

Question 246: You have a client who stands at his workstation on his feet 8-10 hours a day. A PA shows mild increase in thoracic kyphosis, what muscle needs to be strengthened?

a. Rhomboid major
b. Rectus abdominus
c. Pectoralis minor
d. Pectoralis major

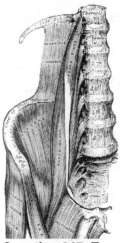

Question 247: Together the iliacus and psoas major form the iliopsoas, they are complete synergists and share three actions of the coxal joint. What are the three actions of these synergists?

a. Extension, ADduction, and Lateral rotation
b. Extension, ABduction, and Lateral rotation
c. Flexion, ADduction, and Lateral rotation
d. Flexion, ABduction, and Lateral rotation

Question 248: Generally this technique rhythmically compresses and releases the tissue and creates kneading and stretching of tissue layers:

a. Light effleurage
b. Petrissage
c. Vibration
d. Lymphatic drainage

Question 249: In 129-199 AD Rome, 16 books on frictions and gymnastics that described the pressure, direction, and frequency of treatment were written by:

a. Buddha
b. Yellow Emperor
c. Galen of Rome
d. Ambroise Pare

Question 250: The theory that massage helps prepare the muscles before sports activity and then removes extra fluid and metabolites after sports activity was also used in:

a. Ancient Greece
b. Renaissance times
c. The Dark ages
d. Ancient Jerusalem

Answers

Question 1: _____ is the study of the functions of an organism?

b. Physiology

Rationale: Physiology is the study of the functions of organisms.

Question 2: A person in the _____ position is lying face up?

b. Supine

Rationale: The person would in the supine body position.

Question 3: Choose from the following the definition of profession?

a. An occupation requiring training and specialized study

Rationale: Profession is defined as: An occupation requiring training and specialized study.

Question 4: Rotation of the head occurs because of this type of joint between the axis and atlas of the cervical vertebrae?

d. Pivot

Rationale: Atlantodontoid; Pivot= designed to allow one bone to rotate around the surface of another (C1=Atlas & C2=Axis). Ellipsoid permits flexion / extension and AB or ADduction, for example the Radiocarpal (wrist) joint.

Question 5: The two joints which create inversion and eversion are:

d. Talocalcaneal (subtalar) and talocalcaneonavicular

Rationale: The talocalcaneal and talocalcaneonavicular joints are modified gliding joints, they function in unison to produce pronation (eversion) and supination (inversion) of the foot.

Question 6: So that therapists can develop a safe and effective treatment plan, it is necessary to have which of the following?

b. Get a complete assessment of client's past and current health history

Rationale: To develop a safe and effective treatment plan, it is best to get a complete assessment and review the client's health history, past and present.

Question 7: The O in the acronym SOAP stands for?

a. Objective

Rationale: The practitioner's observations, testing, and physical findings.

Question 8: To be able to have proper access to the supraspinatus tendon, which positioning would work best?

a. Internally rotating, extending, and ADducting the humerus

Rationale: Positioning the humerus by internally rotating, extending, and ADducting brings the supraspinatus tendon out from under the acromion.

Question 9: A cramp is a:

a. Prolonged muscle spasm

Rationale: Spasm= an involuntary, sustained contraction of a muscle. A cramp is a common or lay term for painful, prolonged muscle spasm.

Question 10: What is the correct order of muscle layers, from superficial to deep, between the thoracic vertebrae and the medial border of the scapula?

d. Trapezius, rhomboids, and ESGs

Rationale: From superficial to deep, the muscles that run in between the thoracic vertebrae and medial border of the scapula are the trapezius, rhomboids, and ESGs (Erector Spinae Group). ESGs next to the spine and ribs, rhomboids are felt throughout the broad superficial trapezius.

Question 11: What muscle would be affected if the area of the superior angle on the scapula was tender to the touch?

d. Levator scapula

Rationale: The superior angle and upper portion of the medial border of the scapula is the insertion for the levator scapula. The best way to palpate the superior angle is to have your client in sidelying position with the scapula superiorly elevated towards the head, its located between the ribs deep to the trapezius. You can feel the superior angle better when it is away from the ribcage.

Question 12: Out of all the muscles that attach to the humeroulnar and humeroradial joints, what muscle would be assessed when flexion is performed?

c. Palmaris longus

Rationale: Flexion of the elbow: biceps brachii, brachialis, brachioradialis, flexor carpi radialis, flexor carpi ulnaris (assists), palmaris longus, pronator teres (assists), extensor carpi radialis longus and extensor carpi radialis brevis (assist). The triceps brachii and anconeus extend the elbow.

Question 13: Each state has varying regulations, which of the following is the best overall definition of scope of practice?

c. The knowledge base and practice parameters of a profession

Rationale: The best definition of scope of practice is the knowledge base and practice parameters of a profession. Each professional has personal limitations as well as professional, they are set up to maintain boundaries that support each profession. It's also ethical to acknowledge limits of practice, freeing ourselves from the belief that we can be all things to all people so we work together with other professionals.

Question 14: What bilateral action does the scalenes group perform?

a. Elevate ribs during inhalation

Rationale: Bilaterally, the scalenes elevate the ribs on inhalation. The anterior fibers bilaterally flex the head and neck. Unilaterally, they all laterally flex the head and neck to the same side and rotate the head and neck to the opposite side.

Question 15: For the effectiveness of the massage, a comfortable balance of communication from both the client and the therapist is:

b. Ideal for treatment

Rationale: Always adjust treatment for each client. Take cues from the client as to the amount of talking that is desired.

Question 16: Hypermobility is a joint dysfunction and defined as:

d. An increased degree of motion at the joint

Rationale: Hypermobility is an increased degree of motion at the joint. Hypomobility is a loss of motion and normal joint play movement at the joint. Temporomandibular joint dysfunction or disorder (TMJD), is a disorder of the muscles of mastication and associated structures. Degenerative disc disease is a degeneration of the annular fibers of the intervertebral disc.

Question 17: Which muscle ADducts the arm?

b. Latissimus dorsi

Rationale: The ADductors of the glenohumeral joint: Latissimus dorsi, teres major, infraspinatus, teres minor, pectoralis major (all), triceps brachii (long head), and coracobrachialis.

Question 18: The linea aspera is on the _____ aspect of the femur?

a. Posterior

Rationale: Vastus Medialis = medial lip of linea aspera. Vastus lateralis = lateral lip of linea aspera. Short head of biceps femoris = lateral lip of linea aspera. All attachment sights on the posterior aspect of the femur.

Question 19: Which ribs are termed the floating ribs?

b. 11 & 12

Rationale: 11&12 are referred to as floating ribs or vertebral ribs with no anterior attachments.

Question 20: The deltopectoral triangle sites of caution consist of:

a. Cephalic vein, clavicular artery, and pectoral nerve

Rationale: The border structures that make up the deltopectoral triangle are the clavicle, deltoid, and pectoralis major and contain the cephalic vein, clavicular artery, and pectoral nerve.

Question 21: What is the name of the two brothers who introduced Swedish Massage to the United States in 1856?

a. Dr. Charles Fayette Taylor and Dr. George Henry Taylor

Rationale: Dr. Charles Fayette Taylor and Dr. George Henry Taylor are the two brothers who introduced the Swedish Movement to the United States in 1856.

Question 22: Tendons are a fibrous tissue that connect:

a. Muscle to bone

Rationale: Tendons are a thick fibrous tissue that connects muscle and bone. Ligaments are a fibrous tissue that connect bone to bone.

Question 23: As a person exhales, the diaphragm will?

d. Relaxes and creates a positive pressure drawing air out the lungs

Rationale: Inhalation (inspiration) expands the chest laterally, elevating the rib cage and depressing/flattening the diaphragm, stretching the lungs and enlarging the thoracic volume, this creates negative pressure to draw air into the lungs. Exhalation (expiration) depresses the chest reducing the lateral dimension of the rib cage and elevating the diaphragm into a dome, relaxing the stretch on the lungs to decrease the volume and raise pressure to draw air out of the lungs.

Question 24: What is a definition of a dual or multidimensional relationship?

c. A relationship that includes a complex and interwoven connection between a massage therapist and another person

Rationale: Dual or multidimensional relationships happen between a massage therapist and another individual that could be a longtime client, neighbor, family member, close friend, business partner, boy/girlfriend, husband, or wife. Boundaries need to be made clear by the massage therapist before a treatment can be done to insure clear expectations for both parties involved.

Question 25: What body system maintains posture, produces body heat, and movement?

b. Muscular

Rationale: The Muscular system produces heat and body movement and maintains posture.

Question 26: To integrate your entire body within your manual manipulations utilizing all your tools, it is best to?

d. All of the above

Rationale: Using a variety of movements, the bodies weight, and proper alignment will help to develop a dynamic application of your mechanics, for successful use and longevity of your body's tools for manual therapy.

Question 27: The hamstring muscles from lateral to medial are?

a. Biceps femoris, semitendenosus, and semimembranosus

Rationale: The head of the fibula on the lateral side is the insertion for biceps femoris, the semitendenosus lies superficial to the wider and deeper semimembranosus.

Question 28: Hyper/hypomobility, TMJD, degenerative disc disease and osteoarthritis are all?

b. Joint dysfunctions

Rationale: Joint dysfunctions: hyper/hypomobility, TMJD, degenerative disc disease, or disorder and osteoarthritis. Postural dysfunctions include; pes planus, iliotibial band contracture, patellofemoral syndrome, hyperlordosis, hyperkyphosis, and scoliosis. Fascial and muscle imbalances may be functional and structural.

Question 29: The main function of the spring ligament is to support the head of which bone?

a. Talus

Rationale: The spring or Plantar Calcaneonavicular ligament stabilizes the medial longitudinal arch, preventing flat foot by supporting the head of the talus.

Question 30: When trying to determine if your client is in the acute or chronic stage of inflammation, when would pain manifest to the affected area?

c. Acute pain is aggravated by activity and when at rest and chronic is only with specific activity

Rationale: Acute pain is aggravated by activity and when at rest Chronic is only with specific activity.

Question 31: The _____ is a strong plantarflexor and crosses both the knee and the ankle joints?

d. Gastrocnemius

Rationale: Gastrocnemius is in charge of flexing the knee and plantar flexion of the ankle. It originates on the posterior surfaces of the femur condyles, inserting on the calcaneus crossing two joints. Soleus does not cross both the knee and ankle joints.

Question 32: What is the purpose of a treatment description?

a. Create informed health care consumers

Rationale: Communicate to client the advantages of the treatment and what they can do after the visit to make lasting differences in their condition.

Question 33: The muscle spindles are proprioceptive nerve receptors or minute sensory organs located in the:

a. Muscle belly

Rationale: Muscle spindles protect the muscle from being overstretched. They monitor muscle length and help control muscle movements by detecting the amount of stretch placed on a muscle.

Question 34: Which of the following causes of wounds is a thermal force?

a. Chemical

Rationale: Causes of wounds: Thermal sources (extreme temperatures, chemical and electrical resulting in a burn). Mechanical forces (trauma, pressure, friction, or sheer forces from an impact between the body and object, or inside body). Types of wounds: Abrasion, laceration, incision, puncture, animal bite, and burns.

Question 35: Of the following effects of hydrotherapy which is not an effect of a heat application?

a. Decrease circulation

Rationale: Hydrotherapy heat effects: Increases in circulation, metabolism, inflammation, respiration, and perspiration. Decreases in pain, muscle spasm, tissue stiffness, and white blood cell production. Hydrotherapy cold application effects: Increases in stimulation, muscle tone, tissue stiffness, white blood cell production, and red blood cell production. Decreases in circulation (primary effect, increase circulation is secondary), inflammation, pain, respiration, and digestive processes. Hydrotherapy ICE applications: Increases tissue stiffness. Decreases circulation, metabolism, inflammation, pain, and muscle spasm.

Question 36: The use of radiography to detect spinal subluxations and misalignment is within which scope of practice?

b. Chiropractic

Rationale: The Chiropractic discipline works with the nervous system in relation to the spinal column and its interrelationship with other body systems. The use of radiography for detection of spinal subluxations and misalignment in order to adjust the related bones and tissues in establishing neural integrity using techniques that work with the inherent recuperative powers of the body. Scope of practice also includes analytic instruments, nutritional advice, and prescribing rehabilitative exercise.

Question 37: _____ is the study of the structure of organisms?

a. Anatomy

Rationale: Anatomy is the study of the structures of organisms.

Question 38: What regulates the body temperature and is known as the thermostat of the body?

c. Hypothalamus

Rationale: Through autonomic nervous system pathways, the hypothalamus continually regulates body temperature around a set point of 96¼ to 100¼ by initiating heat-loss or heat-promoting mechanisms. Also called Homeostasis.

Question 39: What muscle is palpable at the lateral cervical vertebrae and deep to the upper trapezius and is capable of moving the scapula?

b. Levator scapula

Rationale: The levator scapula can be palpated in between the splenius capitis and posterior scalenes. It is the only muscle attached to the lateral cervical vertebrae that is capable of moving the scapula. Actions are: Unilaterally rotating head and neck to same side along with laterally flexing the head and neck, elevation and downward rotation of the scapula. Bilaterally extends the head and neck.

Question 40: What is the best way to access the rhomboid muscles while your client is in the prone position?

b. With their hand in the small of his back

Rationale: The rhomboids major and minor originate on the spinous processes of C7-T5 and inserts on the medial border of the scapula. The best way to access them is to place your clients hand in the small of his back and palpate the fibers that run oblique or at an angle like a christmas tree off the spine deep to the trapezius. Have your client press their elbow up towards the ceiling resisting 30% of their strength, this will tighten the traps as well but you will feel the oblique fibers.

Question 41: To palpate the posterior fibers of the scalenes, what muscles must you go between?

a. Levator scapula and middle scalenes

Rationale: The posterior scalenes are located between the levator scapula and middle scalenes, deep to the other scalenes. Because the belly of this muscle is so small it can be hard to distinguish.

Question 42: Chronic bronchitis results in the production of purulent sputum and is termed a(n):

d. Respiratory pathology

Rationale: Chronic bronchitis lasts at least for three months in a row and over two consecutive years. Respiratory pathologies include: sinusitis, chronic bronchitis, emphysema, and asthma. Peripheral refers to the nervous system outside the central nervous system CNS= brain and spinal cord.

Question 43: Carpal tunnel syndrome (CTS) is a peripheral nervous system condition and is defined as a(n):

a. Condition that results from a compression of the median nerve

Rationale: Carpal tunnel syndrome (CTS) is a condition that results from a compression of the median nerve as it passes through the carpal tunnel in the wrist, resulting in numbness and tingling in the lateral three and one-half digits. Thoracic outlet syndrome (TOS) is a condition that involves compression of the brachial plexus and its accompanying artery between the anterior and middle scalene= anterior scalene syndrome, coracoid process and pectoralis minor= pectoralis minor syndrome and clavicle and first rib= costoclavicular syndrome.

Question 44: Which of the following pathologies is not a musculoskeletal injury?

d. Pes planus

Rationale: Musculoskeletal injuries: Scar tissue, wounds/ burns, contusions, strains, sprains, cruciate/ meniscal injuries, dislocations, fracture, and whiplash. Pes planus is a postural dysfunction.

Question 45: The muscle approximation technique uses the reflex effect of these cells to reduce tone or spasm in a muscle?

c. Muscle spindle

Rationale: Muscle approximation or bringing the ends of the muscle closer together, lessens the stretch on the muscle spindles reducing muscle tone and spasm.

Question 46: What are considered the main supportive components of the nervous system?

b. Neurons

Rationale: Neurons are the main structural component of the nervous system where much of the activity happens.

Question 47: The P in the acronym SOAP stands for?

d. Plan

Rationale: The practitioner's treatment plan, goals, and patient education information.

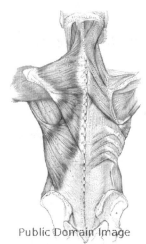

Public Domain Image

Question 48: The Deltoid muscle has groups of fibers that perform different actions; the anterior fibers flex, medially rotate, and horizontally ADduct the glenohumeral joint. The posterior fibers extend, laterally rotate, and horizontally ABduct the glenohumeral joint. What is the one action that all the fibers (anterior, middle, and posterior) are in charge of?

a. ABduction of the glenohumeral joint

Rationale: The Deltoid muscle has anterior, posterior, and middle sectional fibers. The one action they all perform is ABduction. The anterior fibers flex, medially rotate, and horizontally ADduct. The posterior fibers extend, laterally rotate, and horizontally ABduct the glenohumeral joint. The origin is identical to the trapezius insertion, this broad origin and "V" shaped (deltoid) muscle performs every action except ADduction. Because of its size and placement the deltoid is an antagonist to itself in lateral/medial rotation and flexion/extension. These three superficial fibers converge into the deltoid tuberosity insertion on the humerus. The actions of the deltoid only move the glenohumeral joint.

Question 49: Consent to treat is:

c. Required by law for therapists regulated under the health care act

Rationale: The consent to treat or informed consent, is stating that the client understands and agrees to what the therapist is suggesting for treatment.

Question 50: The endocrine system contains?

a. Pituitary, adrenal, and thyroid glands

Rationale: The endocrine system glands; pineal, pituitary, thyroid, parathyroid, thymus, adrenal, pancreas, ovaries, and testes. The endocrine system helps regulate metabolism and is a major body system.

Question 51: In order to locate the insertion site for the temporalis, what is the best action to have your client perform?

c. Clench and relax your jaw

Rationale: With your fingers about an inch superior to the zygomatic arch, have your client contract and relax their jaw. You will feel the temporalis contracting.

Question 52: Asthma is a respiratory pathology that is defined as a(n):

a. Chronic inflammatory disorder with bronchospasms

Rationale: Asthma is a chronic inflammatory disorder with bronchospasms (narrowing of the airways in the lungs), a condition that is reversible over time or following treatment. Sinusitis is a respiratory pathology that is an acute or chronic inflammation of the paranasal sinuses. Chronic bronchitis is a respiratory pathology resulting in the production of purulent sputum for at least three months in a row over a consecutive two years. Emphysema is an enlargement of the air spaces distal to the terminal bronchioles and the destruction of the alveolar walls.

Question 53: To treat trigger points and check for fascial restrictions with Petrissage, what type would be used as an assessment technique?

b. Skin rolling

Rationale: Skin rolling= the skin is lifted between the thumb and fingers and gently rolled over the area being treated or assessed.

Question 54: Osteoarthritis is a joint dysfunction and is defined as:

d. A group of chronic, degenerative conditions that affect the articular cartilage and subchondral bone of joints

Rationale: Osteoarthritis (OA) is a group of chronic, degenerative conditions that affect the articular cartilage and subchondral bone of joints. Hypomobility is a loss of motion and normal joint play movement at the joint. Hypermobility is an increase degree of motion at the joint. Degenerative disc disease is a degeneration of the annular fibers of the intervertebral disc.

Question 55: A new client intake reports they are diabetic, what treatments are contraindicated for this condition?

b. Extreme hydrotherapy and deep cross-fiber friction

Rationale: Deep petrissage, cross-fibre friction and hydrotherapy in extremes are contraindicated because of the possible decreased tissue health and sensory impairments.

Question 56: What muscle extends the arm?

d. Teres major

Rationale: The teres major muscle extends the arm. The teres major and latissimus dorsi are complete synergists. The actions: MAE Medial rotation, ADduction, and Extension of the glenohumeral joint.

Question 57: The muscle's reaction to dysfunction can be categorized into two groups; primarily postural and primarily phasic, which of the following is primarily a postural muscle?

a. Gastrocnemius

Rationale: Primarily postural muscles= shorten in response to dysfunction. Primarily phasic muscles= weaken in response to dysfunction. Primarily postural (short): gastrocnemius, soleus, rectus femoris, biceps femoris, semi sisters, pectineus, ADductors, TFL (Tensor Fasciae Latae), piriformis, iliopsoas, QL (Quadratus Lumborum), ESGs (Erector Spinae Group), diaphragm, intercostals, pec major (clavicular & sternal head), upper trap, levator scap, SCM (Sternocleidomastoid), and wrist and elbow flexors. Primary phasic (weak): peroneals, tibialis anterior, vastus lateralis/medialis, glut max, med & minimus, rectus abdominus, rhomboids, middle/lower traps, serratus anterior, and wrist & elbow extensors.

Question 58: How many curvatures are there in the spine?

c. 4

Rationale: There are 4 curvatures in the spine. Cervical, thorasic, lumbar, and sacral.

Question 59: In order to palpate the contraction of serratus anterior using resistive techniques with your client in supine position, what position should the arm be in?

b. Flexed shoulder with the fist raised to the ceiling

Rationale: The serratus anterior is only superficial under the axilla or armpit between the pectoralis major and latissimus dorsi. It is a well defined muscle in fighters because of the actions it is in charge of: ABduction and depression of the scapula, it also holds the medial border of the scapula tight against the rib cage. With the Flexed shoulder and fist towards the ceiling, you can place one hand on the serratus and the other on the fist. Ask your client to alternate between pushing up towards the ceiling against your 30% resistance and then relaxing.

Question 60: Which of the following occupations is the study of athletic performance, injury prevention, and rehabilitation?

d. Athletic Training

Rationale: Athletic training is defined as the study of athletic performance, injury prevention, and rehabilitation.

Question 61: A _____ is an overlapping alliance that a client and therapist share in addition to the therapeutic relationship.

b. Dual or Multidimensional relationship

Rationale: A Dual or Multidimensional relationship is an overlapping alliance that a client and therapist share in addition to the therapeutic relationship.

Question 62: The cause of Ankylosing spondylitis is idiopathic and defined as:

b. A chronic, systemic inflammatory disorder involving specific areas of the body, primarily the spine

Rationale: Ankylosing (immobility and fixation of joints) spondylitis (inflammation of vertebrae) is a chronic, systemic inflammatory disorder involving specific areas of the body, primarily the spine. Idiopathic (not clearly understood). Peripheral joints (knees and fingers) are also affected. Hyperlordosis is an increase in normal lumbar or lordotic curve and an increase in anterior pelvic tilt/ shortened hip flexors. Hyperkyphosis is an increase in the normal thoracic curve accompanied by protracted scapulae and head-forward posture. Scoliosis is a lateral rotatory deviation of the spine.

Question 63: The muscle that performs opposite actions of the prime mover is an:

d. Antagonist

Rationale: Antagonist, a muscle that performs the opposite action of the prime mover and synergist muscles.

Question 64: To protect your radiocarpal joint when giving a massage, it is best to:

b. Keep your radiocarpal joint in a neutral position

Rationale: Keeping your radiocarpal joint (wrist) in a neutral position helps maintain the strength of your hand and decreases the stress to the joint. Body mechanics / self-care prevents injury in every form of manual therapy.

Question 65: Hydrotherapy is a form of complementary therapy that combines well with massage, one therapeutic use is analgesic which means a(n):

b. Pain relief

Rationale: Analgesic= pain relief or killer can be with hot, warm, and cold applications.

Question 66: Of the following choices, what would be a mechanical force causing a wound?

c. Trauma

Rationale: Causes of wounds: Thermal sources (extreme temperatures, chemical and electrical resulting in a burn). Mechanical forces (trauma, pressure, friction, or sheer forces from an impact between the body and object, or inside body). Types of wounds: Abrasion, laceration, incision, puncture, animal bite, and burns.

Question 67: Which muscle group is located between the SCM and anterior flap of the Trapezius and unilaterally rotates the head and neck to the opposite side?

c. Scalenes

Rationale: Scalenes are sandwiched in between SCM (Sternocleidomastoid) and Trapezius; Splenius Capitis is deep to the Trapezius and Rhomboids rotates the head and neck to the same side.

Question 68: You work in the city and just instructed a co-worker to call 911 while beginning CPR on your unconscious boss, how long do you continue CPR?

d. A doctor or paramedic tells you to stop or takes over

Rationale: It takes about 5-10 minutes for the responders to arrive from the time the call is made. If the scene is determined unsafe and you have started CPR, move them to a safe location and continue CPR. After the call to 911 is made and you commence CPR, you must continue until told to stop by or are replaced by a paramedic or doctor. If you get tired and there is another person available who can do CPR, you can switch. If you are the only person, you must keep going, even if you think it's not helping the victim.

Question 69: Which plane divides the body into right and left halves?

c. Midsagittal

Rationale: Midsagittal or median can be viewed as a midline dividing the body into right and left halves. Sagittal is a vertical cut but not in equal halves. Transverse= horizontal, superior/inferior, and frontal or coronal is anterior/posterior.

Question 70: What is Transference?

a. A biological time machine into childhood emotions

Rationale: Transference was first recognized and recorded by Sigmund Freud. He noticed that clients would have strong feelings and fantasies about him that had no basis in reality. During therapy an emotional nerve is struck by what is said or done to remind the clients of past experiences. These surfacing emotions transfer emotional past and brings psychological needs into the present. So a client's transference reaction to a therapy could mean they are reacting in terms of what they need. This all happens without the client knowing why they have these feelings or react the way they do.

Question 71: When communicating with a client, care is taken not to lead the client or make assumptions about symptoms. What kind of questions are asked to assess the client's conditions?

d. Open-ended

Rationale: Open-ended questions require details from the client about their condition, for a more effective treatment.

Question 72: Which plane divides the body into an upper and a lower portion?

d. Transverse

Rationale: Transverse= horizontal, superior/inferior, and frontal or coronal is anterior/posterior. Midsagittal or median can be viewed as a midline dividing the body into right and left halves. Sagittal is a vertical cut but not in equal halves.

Question 73: If you were talking about the integumentary system, you would be discussing?

b. The skin, nails, hair and sweat glands

Rationale: The skin, nails, hair, sweat and oil glands are all part of the integumentary system.

Question 74: Keeping your hands clean is one of the best ways to prevent the spread of infection and illness in your practice. When is the best time to wash your hands?

a. Before and after a massage

Rationale: Proper hand hygiene is highly important. As healthcare providers we must take standard precautions to reduce risk of infection and communicable diseases. The most effective way is through hand washing before and after each treatment even with the use of gloves and finger cots. The use of waterless hand washing substitutes is good if needed for quick sanitation purposes, but you must wash your hands as soon as you are able. Alcohol-based hand sanitizers can quickly reduce the number of germs on hands in some situations, but sanitizers do not eliminate all types of germs.

Question 75: Which technique is specifically intended to disrupt and break down existing and forming adhesions in muscles, tendons, and ligaments?

b. Cross-fiber friction

Rationale: By using compression and motion the therapist's fingers or thumb do not slide over the skin, instead the superficial tissues are moved over the deeper ones.

Question 76: How many Kilocalories does each gram of fat produce?

a. Nine

Rationale: Kilocalories or Calories are the measured units of energy provided by food.

Question 77: Palpation is always performed _____, starting with the unaffected side.

c. Bilaterally

Rationale: Unaffected tissue is compared to the affected tissue being aware of anatomy and fiber direction.

Question 78: The superficial SCM or sternocleidomastoid is on the lateral anterior aspect of the neck. At its origin it has two heads a sternal and clavicular, and the insertion is the mastoid process and lateral portion of the superior nuchal line on the occiput. Unilaterally it has two actions, bilaterally one. What is the bilateral action of the SCM?

b. Flex the head

Rationale: Bilaterally the SCM or sternocleidomastoid brings the head into flexion. Unilaterally the SCM laterally flexes the head and neck to the same side and Rotates the head and neck to the opposite side. Look at the position of the muscle on each side of the neck. The SCM would work to flex the neck bilaterally, one side could laterally flex the head and neck, but to rotate you would need to active the other side unilaterally. Also bilaterally the SCM assists in inhalation.

Question 79: The glenohumeral joint is freely movable and is functionaly classified as:

c. Diarthrotic

Rationale: Joint Function / Structure: Synarthrotic / Fibrous, Amphiarthrotic / Cartilaginous, Diarthrotic / Synovial. (SAD) Fibrous (S), cartilaginous (A) and Synovial (D).

Question 80: In order to palpate the SITS rotator cuff muscle insertion sites, you must place your thumb and fingers where?

a. Thumb on the lesser tubercle and 2nd-4th finger tips on the greater tubercle

Rationale: The rotator cuff tendons can be palpated best with the client in supine or a seated position. The lesser tubercle is located inferiorly and laterally an inch to the coracoid process. The greater tubercle is located just distal/inferior to the acromion process. You will be able to feel the intertubercular groove lateral to the lesser and medial to the greater. having the thumb on the lesser tubercle and the 2nd-4th finger tips on the greater tubercle will give you the insertions to the SITS. Thumb= subscapularis. 2nd= supraspinatus, 3rd= infraspinatus, 4th= teres minor.

Question 81: What is the most common cause of death among those who have experienced a burn?

b. Sepsis

Rationale: Sepsis is the most common cause of death in those who have been burned because of the increased risk of infection due to the loss of the protective barrier. As a result of deeper burns, an accompanied affect is the immune function is depressed. Periostitis and compartment syndromes produce pain in the lower leg. Hyperkyphosis is the increase in normal thoracic kyphotic curve.

Question 82: In a ninth century temple carving in India, who can be found getting a massage?

b. Buddha

Rationale: Buddha is depicted in a ninth century temple carving in India getting a massage. The Hindi term champna means to press or massage and is highly thought to be the origin of the word shampooing, a word used by English writers to describe a wash, rub, or lathering of the hair.

Question 83: The _____ _____ divides the body into left and right portions.

d. Sagittal plane

Rationale: The descriptive terms medial and lateral are used on this plane along with flexion and extension as actions. Mid-sagittal would be left and right halves, down the mid-line. Sagittal is unequal left and right halves.

Question 84: When a body is divided into anterior and posterior portions, it is called the:

b. Frontal plane

Rationale: Frontal or Coronal plane divides the body into front and back portions. The terms anterior and posterior relate to the frontal plane; actions are ADduction and ABduction.

Question 85: What action can you have your client perform to distinguish between the posterior scalene and levator scapula?

c. Slowly bring your shoulder up toward your ear

Rationale: The best action for palpation is elevation of the scapula or bringing the shoulder up toward the ear. While this action is being performed, place your fingers just anterior to the levator scapula and feel the relaxed posterior scalenes.

Question 86: A summary or outline of standards to which a Massage Therapist agrees to conduct their massage practices with a declaration of acceptable, ethical, and general principles of professional behavior is the _____.

b. Code of Ethics

Rationale: A summary or outline of standards to which a Massage Therapist agrees to conduct their massage practices with a declaration of acceptable, ethical, and general principles of professional behavior is the Code of Ethics. Your school, state, liability insurance, and licensing or certification exams all have a Code of Ethics that are very similar to that which you will need to adhere to. Standards of Practice includes the code of ethics and is specifically defined in regards to Professionalism, legal and ethical requirements, Confidentiality, Business Practices, Roles and boundaries, and Prevention of sexual misconduct. Code of policies and standard of regulations are not terms utilized in massage.

Question 87: You are assessing your clients thumb and find that there is pain on extension and ABduction, what muscle is indicated?

c. ABductor pollicis longus

Rationale: The ABductor pollicis longus performs both extension and ABduction.

Question 88: To properly treat the SCM on a client with left-sided torticollis you can utilize isometric agonist contraction techniques on what directional planes?

a. Lateral flexion and rotation

Rationale: The SCM (Sternocleidomastoid) unilaterally rotates the head and neck to the opposite side and laterally flexes the head and neck to the same side. Torticollis presents head and neck laterally flexed on the affected side (lateral flexion on same side) and the face is turned away from the affected side (opposite side rotation).

Question 89: Generally, any technique applied in a slow, rhythmical, and repetitive manner will evoke a relaxation response and _____.

d. Decrease sympathetic nervous system firing

Rationale: This is facilitated if the techniques are applied in a predictable pattern, at an even rate. Working superficial using light pressure or even using deeper pressure, if applied with a broad surface, such as a full palm or the ulnar boarder of the forearm, can achieve the soothing effect expected from a relaxation massage. Reducing the fight-or-flight response.

Question 90: _____ is the displacement or transfer of latent emotions, thoughts, feelings, and behaviors originally related to childhood experiences that can be triggered by treatment work.

a. Transference

Rationale: Transference is the displacement or transfer of latent emotions, thoughts, feelings, and behaviors originally related to childhood experiences directed at the therapist, that can be triggered by treatment work. Counter-Transference is the practitioner's unresolved emotional issues unconsciously transferred to the client.

Question 91: To reduce symptoms, some massage treatments can be temporarily uncomfortable, such as friction. It is best to:

a. Work within the clients pain tolerance

Rationale: Always adjust treatment to the client's pain tolerance. Communicate that pain is involved but it can be stopped at any time. Using breathwork along with treatments will help decrease pain during treatment and help to relax muscles more effectively. Include self-care for client in the exit interview including water and stretches to help alleviate the possibility of pain after treatment, always discuss the benefits of the treatment.

Question 92: If you cut your finger or have an open hangnail you must use a _____ during the massage.

c. Finger cot

Rationale: Finger cot is the best answer. Would you want a reused glove, nasty band aid, or gauze strip on your body? Protect all involved with proper, comfortable tools.

Question 93: Who is given credit for the invention of Swedish Massage?

c. Per Henrik Ling

Rationale: Per Henrik Ling (1776-1839) founded The Royal Institute of Gymnastics in Stockholm (1813) after developing the Ling Treatment or Swedish Treatment Cure.

Question 94: Which muscle has its insertion at a groove on the clavicle?

d. Subclavius

Rationale: The subclavius muscle has its insertion on the clavicle at the subclavian. The sternocleidomastoid has its origin at the clavicle and the sternum.

Question 95: What body system is in charge of maintaining homeostasis, reproduction, and metabolism?

b. Endocrine

Rationale: The Endocrine System is in charge of homeostasis, development, reproduction, and metabolism through the release of hormones.

Question 96: A slightly movable joint is known as:

a. Amphiarthrotic

Rationale: Joint Function / Structure: Synarthrotic / Fibrous, Amphiarthrotic / Cartilaginous, Diarthrotic / Synovial. (SAD) Fibrous (S), cartilaginous (A) and Synovial (D).

Question 97: When scheduling your client for their next massage, it is better to:

b. Ask for their day and time preference

Rationale: Never show your schedule to your clients, it violates the confidentiality law. Billing insurance without services is fraud and tentatively scheduling only hurts your schedule.

Question 98: Adhesive capsulitis is another name for which pathology?

d. Frozen shoulder

Rationale: Adhesive capsulitis is also known as: frozen shoulder, calcific tendonitis of the rotator cuff, scapulocostal syndrome, subacromial fibrosis, pericapsulitis, or acromioclavicular arthritis. These musculoskeletal conditions are defined as a disorder of the shoulder joint that is caused by the tightening of the joint capsule.

Question 99: When performing a client assessment before treatments, an effective therapist will?

a. Balance the neutral caring approach and the technical investigative approach

Rationale: During assessments it is essential that you gain the trust of the client through your words and observations. Be observant to the client's facial expressions or tensing muscles during testing of a pathology. Don't be afraid to perform an assessment because of pain. Knowing the actions that cause pain, limitations of ROM, willingness of client, and pain tolerance will help to know how to approach treatment. "Please stop the motion when the pain begins and return to neutral" Is used over and over again in active assessments.

Question 100: If your client has a moderate anterior pelvic tilt what three muscles would be shortened?

a. Iliacus, psoas major and rectus femoris

Rationale: Anterior pelvic tilt (downward rotation)= short flexors and long extensors. ASIS pulled inferior.

Question 101: Any repeated activity, occupational or recreational, can lead to an/a:

d. Overuse injury

Rationale: An overuse injury occurs when repetitive microtrauma overloads a tissue's ability to repair itself.

Question 102: Which muscle is also commonly called the "boxer's muscle"?

a. Serratus anterior

Rationale: The serratus anterior muscle is also commonly called the "boxer's muscle" because it ABducts and depresses the scapula making the punching motion possible at the shoulder girdle. It also holds the scapula against the rib cage and if the scapula is fixed it can act in forced inhalation.

Question 103: The cranial sutures are structurally fibrous with no defined movement, what is their functional classification?

a. Synarthrotic

Rationale: Joint Function / Structure: Synarthrotic / Fibrous, Amphiarthrotic / Cartilaginous, Diarthrotic / Synovial. (SAD) Fibrous (S), cartilaginous (A) and Synovial (D).

Question 104: Postural dysfunctions have two classifications, what are they?

c. Structural and functional

Rationale: Structural postural dysfunctions pertains to altered bone shape due to malformation or pathological process. A Functional postural dysfunction pertains to soft tissue such as the muscles, ligaments, tendons and fascia that may be shortened or lengthened.

Question 105: Lymphatic drainage technique reduces:

d. Edema and pain

Rationale: Edema and pain are reduced when the Lymphatic drainage technique is used. Lymphatic massage also reduces the build-up of excess fibrin that can lead to scar tissue.

Question 106: Situated between the posterior scalenes and the splenius capitus is what muscle?

b. Levator scapula

Rationale: Just posterior to the SCM (Sternocleidomastoid) and anterior to the Trapezius on the lateral aspect of the neck, in between the posterior scalenes and the splenius capitus is the levator scapula. It is the only muscle in the lateral cervical vertebrae that moves the scapula. ESGs (Erector Spinae Group).

Question 107: When treating clients who are pregnant or have cardiovascular concerns, it is important to know:

c. The client's blood pressure

Rationale: Because of hypertension it is suggested that the therapist keeps current blood pressure readings and instruct them to get up slowly from the table to prevent post-treatment dizziness.

Question 108: Linda is an IT manager who has been noticing that her team complaints about body pain have been increasing. They have upgraded all the workstations ergonomically, hoping that would take care of the issues. She wants to know if there is a type of massage that could help. Linda would also like her team to be educated on proper posture and alignment in repetitive movements. What modality can you refer her to?

a. Aston-Patterning

Rationale: Aston-Patterning is a treatment system that can transform the quality of life for you and your client. The program includes five steps to specializing a session for your client's unique patterns, specific goals, needs, and interests. Sessions may include massage, movement education, fitness training, postural evaluation, and environmental modifications (i.e. workstations). The five-steps: History, pretesting (walking, standing, sitting, bending, lifting, and reaching), movement education, bodywork (massage, Myo-kinetics, and Artho-kinetics), and ergonomics. Attunement Therapy: Works with physiological elements of relational trauma which are stored in the nervous system. Equine Massage: Horse Massage. Aromatherapy: The science of utilizing highly concentrated extractions from plants to balance, harmonize, and promote the health of the body, mind, and spirit.

Question 109: The resistance of a relaxed muscle to passively stretch or elongate is described as:

b. Muscle tone

Rationale: Muscle tone is the resistance of the muscles and connective tissue to palpation and the active, but not continuous, contraction of muscle response to the stimulation of the nervous system.

Question 110: An example of a long bone would be?

b. The humerus

Rationale: The four bone shapes are long, short (cubed), flat, and irregular. The long bones are any bones in the body that are longer then they are wide. The tibia, fibula, humerus, femur, ulna, radius, clavicle, metacarpals, metatarsals, and the bones in each phalange are long bones. The ribs, cranium, and sternum are flat bones.

Question 111: If you were to start at the anterior flap of the upper trapezius and move anteriorly, what order would you palpate the following muscles?

b. Trapezius, levator scapula, posterior, middle and anterior scalenes

Rationale: The order is trapezius, levator scapula, posterior, middle and anterior scalenes.

Question 112: What two unilateral actions are the scalenes in charge of?

b. Rotation to the opposite side and lateral flexion to the same side

Rationale: Bilaterally, the scalenes elevate the ribs in inhalation. The anterior fibers bilaterally flex the head and neck. Unilaterally, they all laterally flex the head and neck to the same side and rotate the head and neck to the opposite side.

Question 113: What technique is used to reduce edema, ease pain, lower the chance of scar tissue formation, and remove metabolic waste secondary to edema and inflammation?

b. Lymphatic drainage

Rationale: Light, repetitive techniques are used to pump the lymphatic fluid through the superficial lymphatic capillaries. Lymphatic drainage is used in acute and early sub-acute stages to remove excess fibrin that leads to adhesions.

Question 114: If the body is in Homeostasis, it means that the?

c. Body is in a state of equilibrium

Rationale: Homeostasis is used to describe the state of the body's equilibrium or stable internal environment.

Question 115: The autonomic nervous system (ANS) controls?

d. Glands, cardiac, and smooth muscle

Rationale: The autonomic (involuntary) nervous system (ANS) has sympathetic and parasympathetic divisions that control glands, cardiac, and smooth muscle. The Somatic nervous system contains the central nervous system (CNS), peripheral nervous system (PNS), and effector organs.

Question 116: All information given is confidential on a health history intake form unless?

a. The client gives specific written permission

Rationale: State laws vary as to the amount of time you need to keep inactive client information. At any rate you must at all times keep any and all information confidential unless given written permission from client. HCP= Health Care Provider.

Question 117: The A in the acronym SOAP stands for?

b. Assessment

Rationale: The therapist's definition of a suspected condition based off the findings of the subjective and objective sections of SOAP.

Question 118: Relative to its size, this muscle is the strongest muscle in the body, it can manage nearly one hundred-fifty pounds of pressure.

d. Masseter

Rationale: Masseter is the primary chewing muscle; Medial Pterygoid assists the Masseter.

Question 119: With a muscle injury, active free and passive relaxed range of motion are used to assess:

b. Pain in the muscle's range

Rationale: Active free ROM is performed when the client actively contracts the muscles crossing a joint, moving the joint through the unrestricted range. Passive relaxed is performed by the therapist, without the client contracting the muscle. Active and passive test the prime movers. Resistive tests for synergists.

Question 120: The _____ ligament is composed of several ligaments that originate at the medial malleolus. It is designed to protect against medial stress of the talocrural joint?

b. Deltoid

Rationale: Deltoid ligament originates at the medial malleolus and spreads upward into an upside down triangle (deltoid). Spring stabilizes the head of the talus, preventing flat foot. Long plantar is on the plantar aspect of foot and lateral talocalcaneal is on the lateral side.

Question 121: The S in the acronym SOAP stands for?

c. Subjective

Rationale: The patient's perception of the current symptoms and health history.

Question 122: For better exposure of the scalenes, how can you position the head?

d. Rotate head slightly to the opposite side

Rationale: Slightly rotate the head to the opposite side to have better access to the scalenes.

Question 123: The massage profession has many methods that are popular, which of the following is a neuromuscular approach?

a. Reflexology

Rationale: Neuromuscular approaches (nervous or reflexive methods): Neuromuscular techniques, trigger point, reflexology, proprioceptive neuromuscular facilitation, myotherapy, Trager, orthobionomy, strain/counterstrain, and muscle energy techniques (not an all-inclusive list). All other methods are applied kinesiology working with reflexive mechanisms.

Question 124: Your client suffers from hyperglycemia, this is a result of:

d. High blood glucose levels

Rationale: Hypoglycemia= blood glucose levels are too low. Hyperglycemia= excessively high levels of glucose in the blood.

Question 125: What are the 3 types of muscles in the human body?

b. Skeletal, cardiac, and smooth

Rationale: Skeletal, cardiac, and smooth. Skeletal is often referred to as striated and voluntary, where as smooth and cardiac; involuntary.

Question 126: _____ muscle is not under our conscious control and is termed involuntary?

c. Smooth

Rationale: Smooth muscle is involuntary and not under our conscious control.

Question 127: Which of the following forms would you file with the IRS if you had a contract with another company and was paid over $600 for your services?

b. 1099-Misc

Rationale: A 1099-Misc must be filled out with the IRS regarding information for every company. You should receive the filing information from each company before federal taxes are due. A W-9 must accompany the application or first CMS-1500 form to insure proper paperwork procedures.

Question 128: The Standard of Practice in regards to Confidentiality is in respect to:

a. All client information

Rationale: Client confidentiality is a respect of all the client information, and the safeguarding of all forms and records. Disclosure of identifiable information in conversations, advertisements, and legal matters is a breach of confidentiality, a therapist must have the client's written consent to disclose any client information.

Question 129: What forearm muscle would be assessed when both pronation and supination are performed?

b. Brachioradialis

Rationale: The brachioradialis assists in both supination and pronation of the proximal/distal radioulnar joints.

Question 130: When using your CPR/ First aid skills on a suspected stroke victim, you must think:

d. F.A.S.T.

Rationale: F.A.S.T.= Face, ask a person to smile, if there is weakness or drooping on one side of the face. Arm, numbness or weakness in one arm, ask them to raise both arms to check for weakness. Speech, is slurred or trouble getting the words out, ask them to speak a simple sentence to check for slurred or distorted speech. Time, to call 911 if a person has difficulty with any of these tasks.

Question 131: All of the following muscles share the same attachment site:

b. Biceps brachii, Coracobrachialis, and Pectoralis minor

Rationale: The coracoid process of the scapula is the origin of the short head on biceps brachii and the coracobrachialis. This structure also is the insertion for pectoralis minor.

Question 132: As the tissue heals from a wound or burn, modifications of hydrotherapy treatments are required when applying to the affected area because of:

b. Hypersensitivity to temperature extremes

Rationale: Hypersensitivity with newly formed tissue may damage the affected area. With burns, there is also a possibility of the inability to dissipate heat.

Question 133: What are the three phases in acute inflammation?

a. 1: Change in vascular flow, 2: change in vascular permeability and 3: cellular events

Rationale: 1:Change in vascular flow (vasodilation), 2: change in vascular permeability (flood site with WBCs, nutrients and lymph fluid=edema) and 3: cellular events: margination, sticking, diaphedesis, chemotaxis, phagocytosis.

Question 134: Scoliosis is a postural dysfunction and is defined as:

a. A lateral rotatory deviation of the spine

Rationale: Scoliosis is a lateral rotatory deviation of the spine. Hyperlordosis is an increase in normal lumbar or lordotic curve and an increase in anterior pelvic tilt/ shortened hip flexors. Hyperkyphosis is an increase in the normal thoracic curve accompanied by protracted scapulae and head-forward posture. Ankylosing (immobility and fixation of joints) spondylitis (inflammation of vertebrae) is a chronic, systemic inflammatory disorder involving specific areas of the body, primarily the spine.

Question 135: _____ is also known as the master gland?

b. The pituitary gland

Rationale: The pituitary gland is known as the master gland because it manufactures and regulates the hormones that regulate all of the other glands.

Question 136: The best way to locate the intertubercular groove that houses the biceps brachii tendon, is to:

d. Laterally rotate the arm

Rationale: When placing the arm in lateral rotation have your client flex their elbow against slight resistance, you should feel the taut tendon. Make sure they don't flex the shoulder, the deltoid muscles will flex and not allow a proper palpation.

Question 137: If an assessment or diagnosis has already been made for your client it is best to:

b. Achieve your own understanding of the clients' condition

Rationale: For a safe, effective massage therapy treatment it is always best to accumulate your own understanding by performing tests, asking questions, and palpating affected tissue.

Question 138: What structures would be shortened with a chronic varus stress of the tibiofemoral joint?

c. Semimembranosus, semitendinosus and gracilis

Rationale: The semi-sisters (semimembranosus & semitendinosus) and gracilis are shortened in a varus stress. The knees form an "O" or bow-legged leaving the medial aspects shortened and lateral lengthened.

Question 139: The major components of the nervous system are?

b. The spinal cord and brain

Rationale: The major components are the brain and the spinal column.

Question 140: Which of the following pathologies is not a condition of the Peripheral Nervous System?

a. Spinal cord injury

Rationale: Conditions of the Peripheral Nervous System (PNS): Radial nerve lesions, ulnar nerve lesions, median nerve lesions, sciatic nerve lesions, bell's palsy, thoracic outlet syndrome (TOS), carpal tunnel syndrome, and Piriformis syndrome. Spinal cord injury is a CNS or Central Nervous System condition.

Question 141: If your client is suffering from chronic valgus stress, what ligament might be damaged?

b. Medial collateral ligament

Rationale: The MCL= medial (tibial) collateral ligament is a vertical band on the medial aspect of the knee, it attaches to and reinforces the joint capsule (palpable and treatable). It limits lateral rotation and stabilizes against valgus stress. When this ligament tears, it usually tears the joint capsule and medial meniscus as well leaking fluid into the surrounding tissue.

Question 142: What type of joint movement would you use to describe the act of bringing a limb in towards the midline of the body?

b. ADduction

Rationale: ADduction can be described as the act of bringing the limb in towards the midline of the body. ADding to the midline. Moving on a frontal or coronal plane.

Question 143: _____ is a declaration of the general principles of acceptable, ethical, and professional behavior by which massage therapists agree to conduct their practice?

a. Code of ethics

Rationale: Code of ethics= general principles for professional behavior.

Question 144: An Iliotibial band contracture is defined as:

d. A contracture or thickening of the IT band

Rationale: Iliotibial Band contracture is a contracture or thickening of the IT band. Pes planus (pronated foot or flat foot) is a decrease in the medial longitudinal arch and a pronated hindfoot. Iliotibial band friction syndrome is the inflammation and pain at the lateral femoral condyle and IT band juncture. Patellofemoral syndrome is a painful degenerative change to the articular cartilage on the underside of the patella.

Question 145: Which muscle of the leg is involved in the flexion of the thigh?

d. All of the above

Rationale: Flexion of the coxal joint: rectus femoris, ant. gluteus med, gluteus minimus, tensor fascia latae (TFL), sartorius, psoas major, and iliacus. ADductor magnus, longus, brevis, and pectineus assist in flexion.

Question 146: What system in the body regulates and maintains tissue fluids and combats disease?

b. Lymphatic

Rationale: The Lymphatic system removes foreign substances from the lymph and the body, combats disease, absorbs fats, balances, and maintains tissue fluids.

Question 147: To keep your back safe from discomfort or injury while in a massage, you must?

b. Bend at the hip joints

Rationale: Your ball and socket hip joints along with the strong pelvis and leg muscles can easily support your weight, decreasing and relieving the muscles in the back or spinal stress. Keep back, head and neck aligned.

Question 148: To bring the coracoacromial ligament closer to the surface, what action will roll the humeral head anteriorly, pressing the ligament forward?

c. Extension

Rationale: Extending the arm rolls the head of the humerus anteriorly, pressing the coracoacromial ligament forward.

Question 149: What type of ROM testing is used to pinpoint adhesions?

c. Active resisted

Rationale: In AR isometric exercise, the muscle contracts statically or isometricly, without any visible joint motion or muscle shortening. The client contracts the muscle, stress is placed on it, painfully pulling on the adhesion site where the frictions need to be applied in cross-fiber friction. All other answers are not ROM tests. Adson's assesses for thoracic outlet syndrome (TOS). Babinski's tests for spasticity within the central nervous system lesions. Bragard's assesses for meniscal tearing.

Question 150: What three landmarks do you palpate between to find the muscle belly of the deltoid?

d. Acromion, lateral 1/3 of the clavicle and deltoid tuberosity

Rationale: The Acromion, lateral 1/3 of the clavicle and deltoid tuberosity forms a "V" shape on the arm. The deltoid is superficial, you should be able to feel the posterior and anterior fibers.

Question 151: A(n) _____ muscle has the opposite desired action of a _____ muscle.

b. Antagonist/agonist

Rationale: An antagonistic muscle does the opposite actions of the prime mover or agonist muscle. Agonist and prime mover are two terms for the same thing. Agonists are also called prime movers because they permit primary movement of the muscle.

Question 152: Most long nerve fibers are covered with a whitish, fatty material that is called:

c. Myelin

Rationale: Myelin has a waxy appearance that protects and insulates the fibers of the axon to increase the transmission rate of nerve impulses. Dendrites are part of the neuron that extend from the cell body to convey messages TOWARD the cell body.

Question 153: What body system produces blood cells and stores minerals?

c. Skeletal

Rationale: The Skeletal system allows the body to move, produces blood cells, stores minerals, supports and protects all other body systems.

Question 154: What does ABC stand for in first aid/ CPR, when checking an unconscious person?

c. Airway, Breathing, and Circulation

Rationale: The ABC's stand for Airway: open the airway. Breathing: check for movement, and Circulation: check for signs of life.

Question 155: If a client has a subluxation, you would refer them to a:

b. Chiropractor

Rationale: A subluxation is a joint out of alignment and is referred to a Chiropractor. Podiatrist = foot, Nutritionist = Food / health, Acupuncturist = Needle work / Qi (Chi) alignment / Herbologist

Question 156: The endocrine system _____.

d. Produces hormones and secretes them into the blood

Rationale: The endocrine system produces hormones and passes them into the blood stream.

Question 157: When applying deep pressure using your olecranon process or elbow, you must:

a. Use your free hand to palpate and guide it

Rationale: The shoulder and elbow must be in alignment for proper stability with the hand relaxed, to ensure benefits for both the client and MT. Your olecranon process is perfect for applying static and moving pressure to large, thick and strong tissue. Guiding with your fingers or thumb will insure proper receptive abilities.

Question 158: Which of the following choices is part of the endocrine system?

c. Adrenal, gonads, and thyroid

Rationale: The endocrine system glands; pineal, pituitary, thyroid, parathyroid, thymus, adrenal, pancreas, ovaries and testes. Pharynx and larynx are part of the respiratory system.

Question 159: What action is used to assess scapulohumeral rhythm at the scapula or scapulothoracic joint?

d. ABduction

Rationale: Scapulothoracic rhythm is the ratio of motion between the scapulothoracic articulation and the glenohumeral joint, as the arm ABducts through full range. It tests for all joints of the shoulder.

Question 160: What is the definition of contraindication?

d. A symptom or circumstance that makes treatment inappropriate

Rationale: Contraindication (CI)= a symptom or circumstance that makes treatment inappropriate.

Question 161: In postural dysfunctions, the slow twitch postural muscle group:

b. Fatigues slow

Rationale: The postural muscle group has a high amount of slow twitch fibers and muscles fatigue slowly. The phasic muscle group has a high amount of fast twitch fibers and muscles fatigue faster.

Question 162: What muscle is an ADductor of the arm?

c. Coracobrachialis

Rationale: The coracobrachialis muscle is an ADductor of the arm.

Question 163: The _____ is the minimum standard adhered to by a therapist for safe and effective practice.

d. Scope of Practice

Rationale: The Scope of practice is the minimum standard adhered to by a therapist for safe and effective practice.

Question 164: The treatment plan is something developed by the therapist with input from the:

d. All of the above

Rationale: Using information from the client, postural analysis (PA), and range of motion (ROM) testing will help determine the best treatment for the desired result.

Question 165: The Triceps Brachii has one action on the elbow or humeroulnar joint and two actions on the glenohumeral or shoulder joint. What is the one action all three heads perform at the elbow?

a. Extension

Rationale: The Triceps Brachii use all three heads to Extend the elbow (humeroulnar joint). The long head is in charge of extending and ADducting the shoulder (glenohumeral joint). The humeroulnar joint's only actions are flexion and extension.

Question 166: A client presents left-side torticollis, what muscle would be shortened and most effected?

c. Left SCM

Rationale: Torticollis is a condition affecting the head and neck area. The head and neck will be laterally flexed on the affected side and the face will be turned away from the affected side. The SCM (sternocleidomastoid) unilaterally rotates the head and neck to the opposite side and laterally flexes the head and neck to the same side and is the main offender in torticollis.

Question 167: What does the Eustachian tube do?

d. Connects the middle ear with the nasal cavity

Rationale: The Eustachian tube (auditory tube) connects the middle ear (tympanic cavity) with the nasal or nasopharynx cavity serving as a pressure equalizer.

Question 168: With your client prone and the arm at a 90 degree angle hanging off the side of the table, how do you find the muscle belly of the middle fibers of the trapezius?

b. By sliding medially and superior from the spine of the scapula

Rationale: By sliding medially and superior from the spine of the scapula you can feel the middle muscle fibers of the trapezius superficial to the deeper rhomboids and ESGs (Erector Spinae Group).

Question 169: A person who is lying prone would be?

a. On the ventral surface of their body

Rationale: Prone means lying on their stomach or the ventral/anterior part of their body face down.

Question 170: Degenerative disc disease is a joint dysfunction and defined as:

a. A degeneration of the annular fibers of the intervertebral disc

Rationale: Degenerative disc disease is a degeneration of the annular fibers of the intervertebral disc. Hypermobility is an increased degree of motion at the joint. Hypomobility is a loss of motion and normal joint play movement at the joint. Temporomandibular joint dysfunction or disorder (TMJD) is a disorder of the muscles of mastication and associated structures.

Question 171: Leaving a client's health history document lying on the counter during a massage is:

c. Breaching client confidentiality laws

Rationale: Keep your client's personal information in a secure place.

Question 172: Inaccuracies will occur in performing orthopedic testings if:

b. It is repeated too many times

Rationale: When performing tests such as muscle lengthening, applying too many times will begin to stress the muscle and stretch it not just assess it. Or active resistive repeated more then three times can fatigue the muscle and give the appearance of decreased strength.

Question 173: What are the two most popular stances among MT's?

b. The parallel and one-foot forward stance

Rationale: In parallel stance your feet are placed side-by-side and is utilized at the head/foot of the table or facing across the table. The one-foot forward stance is with one foot in front of the other, it is utilized when advancing along the side of the table. The T stance creates rotation at the hip and is not a stable or aligned stance to utilize.

Question 174: Which muscle is responsible for head, neck, and shoulder movements?

d. Trapezius

Rationale: The trapezius is responsible for head, neck, and shoulder movements. It originates on the external occipital protuberance, medial superior nuchal line of the occiput, ligamentum nuchae & C-7 to C-12 spinous processes. The insertion is the lateral 1/3 of the clavicle, the acromion, & scapular spine.

Question 175: What system of the body would help absorb nutrients?

a. Gastrointestinal

Rationale: The gastrointestinal system helps the body absorb nutrients into the bloodstream.

Question 176: What is the best definition for Origin-Insertion Approximation?

c. A passive shortening of the muscle at the musculotendinous junction

Rationale: Origin-Insertion Approximation or O&I is a technique used on cramps or spasm to dissipate the pain. By grasping the muscle at both the origin and insertion, and pushing the musculotendinous or Golgi tendons closer toward the belly of the muscle, and holding this position until the pain is gone. You can also use Reciprocal Inhibition (R/I) and Direct pressure (DP).

Question 177: How many pairs of nerves branch off of the spine?

a. 31

Rationale: There are 31 pairs of nerves branching off of the spine. 8 cervical nerves, 12 thoracic nerves, 5 lumbar nerves, 5 sacral nerves, and 1 coccageal nerve off the spinal cord.

Question 178: As a person inhales, the diaphragm will?

c. Contract and create a negative pressure drawing air into the lungs

Rationale: Inhalation (inspiration) expands the chest laterally, elevating the rib cage and depressing/flattening the diaphram, stretching the lungs and enlarging the thoracic volume, this creates negative pressure to draw air into the lungs. Exhalation (expiration) depresses the chest, reducing the lateral dimension of the rib cage and elevating the diaphragm into a dome, relaxing the stretch on the lungs to decrease the volume and raise pressure to draw air out of the lungs.

Question 179: Which of the following massage profession methods is an approach of applied kinesiology?

d. Touch of health

Rationale: Applied kinesiology (works mostly with reflexive mechanisms): Touch of health, three-in-one concepts, applied physiology, and educational kinesiology (not an all-inclusive list). All other methods are Energetic (biofield) approaches that initiate the reflexive response.

Question 180: The "Yellow Emperor's Classics of Internal Medicine", China's oldest Medical book, contained massage treatments for:

d. Paralysis and reduced circulation

Rationale: The "Yellow Emperor's Classics of Internal Medicine", China's oldest Medical book, contained massage treatments for Paralysis and reduced circulation.

Question 181: Which of the following body systems is in charge of muscular development?

d. Endocrine system

Rationale: The endocrine system releases growth hormone to insure normal muscle development. Thyroxine and catecholamine hormones regulate muscle metabolism. The muscular activity promotes catecholamine release and muscles mechanically protect endocrine glands.

Question 182: Which of the following is not part of the upper respiratory system?

d. Trachea

Rationale: Upper= Nostril, nasal cavity, oral cavity, pharynx, and larynx (vocal cords). Lower= Trachea, primary bronchi, lungs, and diaphragm.

Question 183: Which muscle has its origin at the aponeurotic fibers of the iliolumbar ligament and the iliac crest?

c. Quadratus lumborum

Rationale: The quadratus lumborum muscle has its origin at the aponeurotic fibers of the iliolumbar ligament and at the adjacent portions of the iliac crest.

Question 184: In anatomical position, which bone of the forearm is lateral?

a. Radius

Rationale: In anatomical position the radius is the bone of the forearm that is lateral, the ulna is medial.

Question 185: The superficial pectoralis major is divided into three sections; clavicular, sternal, and costal fibers. This muscle also is an antagonist to itself with its upper and lower fibers. What are the actions of the upper fibers?

d. Flexion and horizontal ADduction of the glenohumeral joint

Rationale: The pectoralis major has clavicular, sternal, and costal fibers. These three sections work together to ADduct, medially rotate (the glenohumeral joint), and assist in elevation of the thorax with forced inhalation. The upper fibers flex and horizontally ADduct the glenohumeral joint. The lower fibers extend the glenohumeral joint, making this muscle an antagonist to itself.

Question 186: Decreasing muscle spasm and increasing the resting length of muscles is an effect of:

a. Mechanical stimulation of golgi tendon organs

Rationale: The golgi tendon organs are proprioceptive nerve receptors located in the tendons near the junction with the muscle. Mechanical stimulation will help decrease muscle spasm and increase the resting length of an acute injury.

Question 187: The insertion of needles and the application of moxibustion is within which of the following occupation's scope of practice?

c. Acupuncture

Rationale: Acupuncture is a form of primary health care that is based on traditional Chinese medicine. It is used to promote, restore, and maintain health to prevent disease. Many adjunctive therapies are used to diagnose and treat including but not limited to the insertion of needles and applying moxibustion (herbs burned near the skin).

Question 188: Which of the following muscles attach to the IT band?

b. Tensor fascia latae

Rationale: The IT (Iliotibial) band is the insertion to the TFL and gluteus maximus.

Question 189: Of the following pathologies, what is not a respiratory condition?

c. Hemiplegia

Rationale: Respiratory pathologies: Sinusitis, chronic bronchitis, emphysema, and asthma. Hemiplegia is a CNS or

Central Nervous System condition.

Question 190: What is the main portion or the shaft of the bone called?

d. Diaphysis

Rationale: The Diaphysis is the main shaft or largest portion of the bone. It is composed of compact bone and contains (in adults) the yellow bone marrow. In infants it is the site for forming blood cells and red bone marrow.

Question 191: The abdomen can be separated into four quadrants, which of the following is within the left lower quadrant (LLQ)?

a. Sigmoid colon and left ovary/ tube

Rationale: RUQ: LiveR, gallbladdeR, duodenum, pancreas, right kidney, and hepatic flexure. RLQ: Cecum, appendix, and right ovary/ tube. LUQ: Stomach, spleen, left kidney, pancreas, and splenic flexure. LLQ: Sigmoid colon and left ovary/ tube.

Question 192: Your client sits at a computer for more than 10 hours a day Monday through Friday, what five muscles of the hip and thigh are shortened?

c. Iliacus, psoas major, rectus femoris, sartorius and gluteus medius

Rationale: When in a sitting position, the hip flexors are shortened: Iliacus, psoas major, rectus femoris, sartorius and gluteus medius (anterior fibers). Lengthened extensors: Gluteus maximus, biceps femoris, semitendinosus, semimembranosus and gluteus medius (posterior fibers).

Question 193: A lack of vitamin D, pain resulting from inflammation, and direct or indirect trauma of infection can cause:

b. Muscle spasm and cramps

Rationale: Spasm= an involuntary, sustained contraction of a muscle. A cramp is a common or lay term for painful, prolonged muscle spasm. Vitamin D helps to make enzymes that transport calcium which is necessary for normal muscle contractions. TPs are caused by mechanical or postural stresses.

Question 194: Branches of the brachial plexus and subclavian artery pass through what two muscles?

d. Anterior and middle scalenes

Rationale: The anterior and middle scalenes have a little passageway for the brachial plexus and subclavian artery.

Question 195: What term is indicated when a client becomes emotional after meeting with their MT because their MT resembles a relative that has just passed away?

a. Reflexive

Rationale: A reflexive response happens when fragile feelings are present because of situations or memories. Ask if alone time is needed before the massage begins or if they need to reschedule. They may also need the option, if available, to request another therapist.

Question 196: As a reaction to the presence of foreign particles, the body's immune system may create?

c. Antibodies

Rationale: As a reaction to antigens (toxins, bacteria, and foreign proteins), the body may activate the immune system to create antibodies or immunoglobulins (Igs).

Question 197: What two actions are most frequently restricted significantly and are painful in Frozen shoulder conditions?

a. ABduction and external rotation

Rationale: Frozen shoulder is a painful overuse injury with significant restriction of the active and passive ROM at the shoulder affecting ABduction and external rotation.

Question 198: What is Projection?

b. Applying your own current feelings, emotions, or motivations onto another person

Rationale: Projection of your current feelings, emotions, or motivations onto another person without realizing your reaction is really more about you than it is about the other person. Some people also refer to projection as a transference. However transference deals with childhood emotions clouding rational reactions, not the current reaction, to a fight just prior to a therapy session. Massage Therapists can not diagnose.

Question 199: Where can you find the temporal bone?

c. Skull

Rationale: It is located on the left and right sides of the skull connecting with the zygomatic bones.

Question 200: Brandon is a pitcher and has recently been given a diagnosis of carpal tunnel syndrome from his team doctor. He would like to do everything in his power to get rid of this pain so he can avoid surgery. He has two more years on his scholarship and would like to keep it. Massage has been helping with a reduction in his pain, but he still needs to improve before he can be given the green light to pitch again. He has taken a month off of training in the off-season and would like to know if there is anything additional he could be doing. What technique would you refer Brandon to in order to gain a better understanding of his posture and alignment to avoid surgery?

d. Alexander Technique

Rationale: The Alexander Technique promotes education in movement to improve posture and adjust conditioned patterns of movement. An Australian actor named F. M. Alexander in the 1800s developed this technique. He discovered that misuse of the neuromuscular activity of the head, neck, and spine caused maladaptive functioning and found that this could be corrected. Amma: TCM Deep Massage working with meridians. Acupressure: TCM finger or knuckle pressure working along the meridians. Active Isolated Stretching: Athletic stretching method used to lengthen muscles and release the fascia.

Question 201: For treatment of a repeat client it is best to:

c. Review the client's health history (HH)/SOAP's and request feedback on effects of the treatment

Rationale: It is necessary that you ask about any changes that may have occurred in health status for proper treatment.

Question 202: What is the anatomical word for collar bone?

d. Clavicle

Rationale: Clavicle, part of the appendicular shoulder complex.

Question 203: When assessing the radiocarpal joint, what muscle group would you lengthen to release or decrease mild extension at the wrist?

a. Extensors

Rationale: Relax the prime movers= extensors of the radiocarpal joint; Extensor carpi radialis longus/brevis, extensor carpi ulnaris and extensor digitorum.

Question 204: The tibialis anterior and fibularis (peroneus) longus support the:

c. Transverse arch

Rationale: The transverse arch is a side-to side concavity on the underside of the foot. The support of the anatomical stirrup (fibularis (peroneus) longus and tibialis anterior) helps prevent the collapse of the transverse arch.

Question 205: What bone in the body does not articulate with other bones?

b. Hyoid

Rationale: The hyoid is the only bone in the body that does not articulate with other bones. It is suspended by ligaments and tendons. It is supported by the muscles of the neck and in turn is the root of the tongue.

Question 206: What is the best position to palpate the superior angle of the scapula?

c. Sidelying with scapula superiorly elevated towards the head

Rationale: The best way to palpate the superior angle is to have your client in sidelying position with the scapula superiorly elevated towards the head, its located between the ribs deep to the trapezius. You can feel the superior angle better when it is away from the ribcage. Insertion of the Levator scapula.

Question 207: To breakdown adhesions that prevent normal motion, this technique can be used in sub-acute and chronic stages of healing?

d. Cross-fiber friction

Rationale: Adhesions may be within muscle fibers and between structures such as ligaments and tendons. Over multiple treatments breaking-down adhesions helps to form smaller, more mobile scarring, helping the alignment of the collagen fibers.

Question 208: When using your thumb without reinforcements you must:

c. Keep it in line with the radius

Rationale: The thumb has many advantages over your fingers. It has one less interphalangeal joint and it is larger making it more stable and stronger with a wide range of motion due to the carpometacarpals joint. Like all other tools, alignment is essential. It can be used without being reinforced but not for long. For long periods of pressure reinforce it with a soft open or closed fist or your other hand to protect and stabilize the joints.

Question 209: What are the four "T"s of palpation?

b. Temperature, tone, tenderness, and texture

Rationale: Temperature may be hot indicating inflammation or cold for ischemia. Tone being hyper or hypotonic relative to nearby muscles. Tenderness may be pain, tenderness, or unusual sensations. Texture; edema or swelling, healthy tissue has even texture.

Question 210: Which of the following body systems is in charge of regulating body temperature and transporting nutrients / hormones?

c. Circulatory

Rationale: The Circulatory System transports hormones, waste products, nutrients, and gases. As well as regulating body temperature and the immune system.

Question 211: A(n) _____ compression is a static compression applied by the therapist's thumbs, fingertips, or olecranon to a trigger point?

d. Ischemic

Rationale: A trigger point is a hyperirritable spot, usually within a taut band of skeletal muscle or its fascia. While staying within the client's pain tolerance, the pressure used is sufficient to temporarily cause local ischemia in the tissue.

Question 212: _____ is the study and development of a particular skill or professional knowledge base associated and applied within a scope of practice.

c. Competency

Rationale: Competency is the study and development of a particular skill or professional knowledge base associated and applied within a scope of practice.

Question 213: Which one of the following would the parasympathetic nervous system control?

c. Slowing down the heart; intestinal activity

Rationale: The parasympathetic is responsible for slowing the heart rate while the sympathetic would do the opposite and speed it up.

Question 214: What is the bony landmark on the humerus that houses the forearm flexors?

c. Medial supracondylar ridge

Rationale: The medial supracondylar ridge is the origin for the flexor muscles of the forearm. Most text books and instructors list the medial epicondyle as the origin. This question is designed to help you choose the best possible answer.

Question 215: Which system of the body would regulate the blood pH and exchange gases?

d. Respiratory

Rationale: The Respiratory System regulates blood pH levels and exchanges gases, Oxygen, and Carbon Dioxide.

Question 216: If a client comes to you with a headache that has referred pain, it is most likely a:

b. Tension headache

Rationale: Tension headaches have bilateral pain, migraine, cluster and chronic paroxysmal hemicrania have unilateral pain. Tension headaches are caused by trigger points with referral pain.

Question 217: While it is regrettable, transference does happen during treatments. If you encounter a client who has experienced a negative childhood emotion and transferred an irrational reaction towards you, it is best to:

b. Allow the client to be informed of the transference and possibility give them the option of ending the session or having a moment to themselves. Always respect the clients needs (within reason)

Rationale: Not taking a reaction personally is important. Transference reactions aren't always recognized right away. Thinking logically with a rational conclusion will help you to realize not everything is about you. Take extra care not to counter-transfer your past emotional reactions to the transference that is expressed by your client.

Question 218: What two muscles ADduct the scapula?

b. Rhomboids and trapezius (middle fibers)

Rationale: ADduct or retraction= Trapezius (middle fibers) and Rhomboid major and minor.

Question 219: Thoracic outlet syndrome (TOS) is a peripheral nervous system condition defined as a(n):

d. Condition that involves compression of the brachial plexus

Rationale: Thoracic outlet syndrome (TOS) is a condition that involves compression of the brachial plexus and its accompanying artery between the anterior and middle scalene= anterior scalene syndrome, coracoid process, and pectoralis minor= pectoralis minor syndrome and clavicle and first rib= costoclavicular syndrome. All other conditions are CNS. Cerebral palsy (CP) is a motor function disorder resulting from damage to the immature brain. Parkinson's is a Progressively diminishing basal ganglia function resulting in slow, increasingly difficult movement, accompanied by resting tremors and muscular rigidity. Multiple sclerosis (MS) is a condition where demyelination of the nerves occurs.

Question 220: Plantar fasciitis is an inflammation of the plantar fascia and termed an:

a. Overuse injury

Rationale: Plantar fasciitis is an overuse injury resulting in inflammation of the plantar fascia. Other overuse conditions include: periostitis/ compartment syndrome, tendonitis, bursitis, and frozen shoulder.

Question 221: Which of the following pathologies is not a condition of the Central Nervous System?

b. Radial nerve lesions

Rationale: Conditions of the Central Nervous Systems (CNS): Communication skills, ambulation aids, decubitus ulcers, seizures, hemiplegia, multiple sclerosis, Parkinsons, cerebral palsy, spinal cord injury, and poliomyelitis. Radial nerve lesions is a peripheral nervous system condition.

Question 222: What body system detects sensations and controls movements?

a. Nervous

Rationale: The Nervous System controls all physiological and intellectual movements. It also detects bodily sensations and controls every physical move the body makes.

Question 223: While your client is seated, what position should the arm be in to be able to feel the antagonistic abilities of the posterior and anterior deltoid fibers?

a. Arm at their side with elbow flexed

Rationale: While placing your right hand on the deltoid, shake hands with your clients left hand. Make sure the elbow is at their side then ask them to medially and laterally rotate the arm against 30% resistance. The anterior fibers contract with medial rotation and the posterior fibers with lateral rotation.

Question 224: Using your palm allows for a broader surface contact, which of the following positions is correct?

a. Maintain wrist joint and forearm alignment with fingers and thumb relaxed

Rationale: The entire palmer surface is an effective tool for superficial and deep strokes or palpation. It is a broad surface with added support of the fingers and thumb.

Question 225: Which of the two lower leg bones is the largest?

d. Tibia

Rationale: The tibia or shin bone is the largest out of the tibia and fibula.

Question 226: The Gluteus Medius has anterior and posterior fibers, what actions are the anterior fibers in charge of?

b. Flexion and medial rotation of the coxal joint

Rationale: The Gluteus Medius has two sections of fibers, the anterior and the posterior. The anterior medius (AM) is in charge of (FM) Flexion and Medial rotation. The posterior fibers are the exact opposite, extension and lateral rotation. Both the anterior and posterior ABduct the coxal joint. Just like the Deltoid muscle the Gluteus Medius is an antagonist to itself in flexion/extension and medial/lateral rotation, plus all the fibers ABduct.

Question 227: Which of the following choices would the sympathetic nervous system control?

b. Constriction of blood vessels

Rationale: Constriction of blood vessels and increased blood pressure are results of stimulus to the sympathetic nervous system. Slowing down the heart and respiratory rate would come from stimulation of the parasympathetic.

Question 228: Sebaceous glands are found in which layer of tissue?

c. Dermis

Rationale: The epidermis (epithelium) is the tough protective layer that is avascular (no blood supply or nerves). Strata layers, deep to superficial; stratum basale, spinosum, granulosum, lucidum, and corneum. The dermis is rich in blood vessels the dense connective tissue layers; upper papillary and deep reticular, also contains nerves.

Question 229: Multiple sclerosis (MS) is a condition that causes demyelination of nerves, it is termed a:

b. Condition of the CNS

Rationale: Conditions of the Central Nervous Systems (CNS): Communication skills, ambulation aids, decubitus ulcers, seizures, hemiplegia, multiple sclerosis, Parkinsons, cerebral palsy, spinal cord injury, and poliomyelitis. MS is a result of scar tissue formations affecting the nerve transmission in scattered areas of the spinal cord and brain.

Question 230: When a therapist files all applicable state and federal taxes, they are following the Standard of Practice under which section?

b. Business Practices

Rationale: Business Practices covers the therapist's professional role in regards to integrity, honesty, and lawfulness pertaining to the guidelines set forth in the profession.

Question 231: Who can request health history information without written consent of the client?

c. Anyone by Court Order

Rationale: The only time you can let anyone, other than your client, see your intake and SOAP forms, is if you have been given a court order. Then you are required by law to produce all documents required. In any other case there must be a written consent.

Question 232: A spasm is:

c. An involuntary, sustained contraction of a muscle

Rationale: Spasm= an involuntary, sustained contraction of a muscle. A cramp is a common or lay term for painful, prolonged muscle spasm.

Question 233: A functional postural dysfunctions:

c. Can be altered by working with the soft tissue and fascia

Rationale: Structural postural dysfunctions pertains to altered bone shape due to malformation or pathological process. A Functional postural dysfunction pertains to soft tissue such as the muscles, ligaments, tendons and fascia that may be shortened or lengthened. Massage can help with functional but not the structural.

Question 234: Of the following choices, which is the best that defines professionalism?

d. The adherence to professional status, methods, standards, and character

Rationale: Professionalism is the adherence to professional status, methods, standards, and character.

Question 235: When you treat each client with dignity, respect, and worth, you are adhering to which Standard of Practice?

b. Professionalism

Rationale: The Professional standards of massage encompass compassionate, responsible, and respectful touch to promote healing and well-being and support optimal levels of professional practice.

Question 236: Which system eliminates waste from the circulatory system and balances water within the body?

c. Urinary

Rationale: The Urinary System balances water and ions, removes waste, and regulates blood pH.

Question 237: If your client has a moderate posterior pelvic tilt what three muscles would be lengthened?

b. Iliacus, psoas major and rectus femoris

Rationale: Posterior pelvic tilt (upward rotation)= short extensors an long flexors. ASIS (Anterior Superior Iliac Spine) pulled superior.

Question 238: Piriformis syndrome is a peripheral nervous system condition and is defined as a(n):

b. Compression of the sciatic nerve

Rationale: Piriformis syndrome is a compression of the sciatic nerve by the piriformis muscle. Carpal tunnel syndrome (CTS) is a condition that results from a compression of the median nerve as it passes through the carpal tunnel in the wrist, resulting in numbness and tingling in the lateral three and one-half digits. Thoracic outlet syndrome (TOS) is a condition that involves compression of the brachial plexus and its accompanying artery between the anterior and middle scalene= anterior scalene syndrome, coracoid process and pectoralis minor= pectoralis minor syndrome and clavicle and first rib= costoclavicular syndrome.

Question 239: You have performed a postural assessment on your client who was in a marathon three days ago, both legs have mild lateral rotation, what muscle would be short and hypertonic?

c. Piriformis

Rationale: Lateral or external rotation indicates that the lateral rotators are tight. A tight piriformis can also endanger the sciatic nerve. Another major muscle for lateral rotation is the Gluteus maximus (all fibers).

Question 240: In the 1932 Dr. Emil and Estrid Vodder develop what technique?

b. Manual Lymphatic Drainage

Rationale: In 1932 Dr. Emil and Estrid Vodder of France developed Manual Lymphatic Drainage.

Question 241: To prevent infectious and communicable diseases the simplest, most effective way to minimize risk is hand washing. The CDC has four steps for proper hand washing. What is the fourth step?

a. Dry hands with a paper towel

Rationale: Proper hand washing technique is; #1. Apply soap to hands. #2. Rub hands together for at least 20 seconds to work up a lather. Pay particular attention to scrubbing the backs of your hands, between your fingers, and under your nails. #3. Rinse hands using warm water. #4. Dry hands with a paper towel. Use the paper towel to turn off the faucet, the light, and open the door before placing the towel in the garbage. http://www.cdc.gov/Features/HandWashing/

Question 242: What muscle would you be assessing with a severe downward rotation of the scapulothoracic joint?

c. Levator scapula

Rationale: Downward rotation of the scapulothoracic joint= Levator scapula, rhomboid major and minor.

Question 243: The connective tissue within the medullary cavity is called?

b. Bone marrow

Rationale: Bone marrow is the connective tissue in the medullary cavity of the bone.

Question 244: A _____ is a limit that is adhered to in order to separate and protect the integrity of all parties involved.

c. Boundary

Rationale: A Boundary is a limit that is adhered to in order to separate and protect the integrity of all parties involved.

Question 245: What system of the body removes waste from the circulatory system?

a. Urinary

Rationale: The Urinary System not only removes waste from the circulatory system it also helps regulate proper pH and ion balance.

Question 246: You have a client who stands at his workstation on his feet 8-10 hours a day. A PA shows mild increase in thoracic kyphosis, what muscle needs to be strengthened?

a. Rhomboid major

Rationale: Kyphosis shortens the anterior muscles and stretch weakens the posterior (thoracic) muscles. The pectoralis minor should be lengthened first opening up the shoulder girdle, relaxing the hypotonic short and releasing the stretch on the lengthened muscles.

Question 247: Together the iliacus and psoas major form the iliopsoas, they are complete synergists and share three actions of the coxal joint. What are the three actions of these synergists?

c. Flexion, ADduction, and Lateral rotation

Rationale: These important hip flexors also stabilize the lower back. They are partially accessible deep to the abdomen. The three actions are: flexion, ADduction, and lateral rotation. The psoas major stretches from the anterior bodies and transverse processes of the lumbar to the lesser trochanter. The iliacus originates on the iliac fossa and also inserts on the lesser trochanter of the femur. Looking at the placement of the attachment points and the directions of the fibers it is easy to tell that these muscles are not capable of extension or ABduction.

Question 248: Generally this technique rhythmically compresses and releases the tissue and creates kneading and stretching of tissue layers:

b. Petrissage

Rationale: Petrissage= French meaning to knead, these terms are often used interchangeably. This technique is used after the tissue is warmed up because of the increased pressure and focus of Petrissage.

Question 249: In 129-199 AD Rome, 16 books on frictions and gymnastics that described the pressure, direction, and frequency of treatment were written by:

c. Galen of Rome

Rationale: Galen of Rome wrote 16 books on frictions (massage) and gymnastics (remedial exercise) that described the pressure, direction, and frequency of treatment in 129-199 AD.

Question 250: The theory that massage helps prepare the muscles before sports activity and then removes extra fluid and metabolites after sports activity was also used in:

a. Ancient Greece

Rationale: In ancient Greece, a Greek physician Asclepides used massage, exercise, and hydrotherapy with the theory that massage helps prepare the muscles before sports activity and removes extra fluid and metabolites after sports activity.

CPSIA information can be obtained at www.ICGtesting.com
Printed in the USA
LVOW09s1020090614

389216LV00009B/76/P